Marjorie O'Harra

SOUTHERN OREGON

short trips into history

Although no attempt has been made to present
a comprehensive history of Southern Oregon in
this collection, the stories have been arranged, in
as far as is possible, in chronological order.

Published by the Southern Oregon Historical Society, Jacksonville, Oregon.

© 1985 Marjorie Lutz O'Harra
All rights reserved. Made in U.S.A.
Library of Congress Catalogue
ISBN 0-943388-06-6

CONTENTS

45514

BUCKHORN MINERAL SPRINGS

Buckhorn Springs Road.

BUCKHORN MINERAL SPRINGS

Spring or fall is the best time of year to enjoy the Buckhorn Springs Road and the beauty of the narrow Emigrant Creek valley in the foothills of the Siskiyou and Green Springs mountains.

Here you will find green fields and split rail fences, tall oaks and wildflowers growing in profusion on the banks of Emigrant Creek. If you enjoy fresh air and country smells, it is pleasant to park and walk a mile or two along the flat, graveled road.

This road was part of the Applegate Trail into the southern part of the Oregon Territory (see page 17) and later it was used by stagecoaches and freight wagons traveling between the Rogue River Valley and the Klamath country. The Dozier Century Farm (1876-1976) is here. Wagner Soda Springs, a stage stop in the 1880s and a mineral water resort and bottling works, also stood alongside this road.

But for the moment, back to the early days.

TO THE INDIANS, A SACRED PLACE

Long ago, before white men came to the valleys of the Siskiyous, Indians made hi-u-skookum medicine in the canyon Emigrant Creek cut through the mountains east of Ashland, at a place later known as Buckhorn Mineral Springs.

The Indians attributed the springs and their virtues to the Great Spirit. They believed the gas that escaped from the water was the breath of the Great Spirit and that it would cure afflictions or persons who led worthy lives. By the same token, the gas meant certain death for the unworthy.

Gas escapes through fractures in the underlying rock in the springs area. At these fractures the Indians hollowed out shallow pits and lined them with boughs. Those brought for treatment were placed in the pits to remain under watchful eyes until they fell unconscious, then they were removed to a tent where their limbs were rubbed and manipulated until they regained consciousness. They were given teas and mineral water to drink, and they received the incantations of the medicine man. This treatment was repeated for several days until the patients were deemed well or prepared for burial.

The Indians insisted the treatment seldom failed to cure even the most obstinate cases of rheumatism, asthma, kidney disease and stomach trouble — if the striken person was worthy of continued life. Dead birds, squirrels, snakes and other small animals and reptiles often were found in the pits, a reminder that carbonic acid gas, the "breath of the Great Spirit," should be used with caution.

Even when the tribes of the Land of Many Lakes were at war with the Rogue Valley tribes, Modoc and Klamath Indians knew they could strap their sick on ponies and take them to the place of healing waters. They were not molested once they reached the springs. The place where the Great Spirit chose to administer the benefits of his healing breath was considered sacred by the Indians.

Although many mineral springs can be found in the Siskiyou mountains of Southern Oregon and Northern California, the Indian legend that originated in a time long forgotten placed faith only in the healing properties of those now known as Buckhorn Mineral Springs.

The Buckhorn Mineral Springs Resort was developed in the early 1900s by white promoters of "healing waters." The property now is in private ownership and not open to the public.

To reach Buckhorn Springs Road and the Emigrant Creek valley, follow Oregon 66 nine miles east of Ashland. Buckhorn Springs Road intersects from the right and is well marked. Two miles from this junction the road forks. You can continue on Tyler Creek Road, which brings you back onto Oregon 66 just below Green Springs summit, but the road is not regularly maintained and may be rough. For a short, pleasant trip, turn around at the fork and retrace the route home.

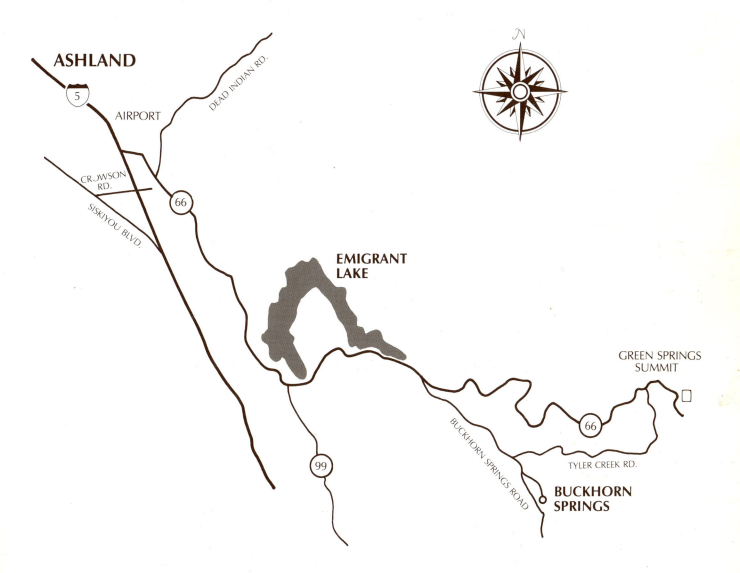

ASHLAND

5

AIRPORT

DEAD INDIAN RD.

CROWSON RD.

66

SISKIYOU BLVD.

EMIGRANT LAKE

99

BUCKHORN SPRINGS ROAD

66

GREEN SPRINGS SUMMIT

TYLER CREEK RD.

BUCKHORN SPRINGS

N

THE APPLEGATE TRAIL AND INTERSTATE 5

A ribbon of highway makes travel fast and easy today.

THE APPLEGATE TRAIL AND INTERSTATE 5

As you drive along Interstate 5, the broad ribbon of highway that makes travel through Oregon so fast and easy today, you are tracing the route of the Applegate Trail.

The Applegate Trail was established in 1846 to offer pioneer families who were coming to settle the Oregon Territory an alternative to the difficult Oregon Trail.

This story of the exploration of the Applegate Trail is based on the journal kept by Lindsay Applegate.

LINDSAY APPLEGATE'S VOW

Staring into the frothing whirlpool and the gray-green waters of the Columbia River, Lindsay Applegate vowed that he would find a better, safer route for others who would come to settle the Oregon Territory.

Lindsay Applegate had just helplessly witnessed the drowning of his ten-year-old son Warren, his nephew, and a man named McClelland, who died after a desperate struggle for life in the river. Three others who were on the raft that vanished in the whirlpool had been rescued.

The Applegate brothers, Lindsay, Charles and Jesse, and their families were with the Great Migration of 1843, Lindsay the soldier, Charles the counselor, and Jesse, captain of the famous Cow Column.

Theirs was the largest wagon train yet to make the trek west and it had been plagued by hard travel. The guides searched the mountains for passes that would accommodate the wagons. The men cut their way through dense forests, and creeks and gullies were crossed by pack trails.

By the time they reached the upper Columbia River, the teams were exhausted. The Applegates and several other families decided to leave the animals at the Hudson Bay Company outpost and go down the Columbia by water. With whipsaw and a few crude tools, the men lashed driftwood and logs together to build rafts on which they loaded the contents of the wagons. With two Indian guides, the emigrants started the long, dangerous trip.

And now it appeared the heartaches had only just begun. Survivors of the river tragedy had no burial to perform. The bodies lost in the whirlpool could not be found.

But the emigrants had no time to linger in grief. It was November and the party must reach Jason Lee's mission in the Willamette Valley before winter. With heavy hearts the travelers packed their supplies on their backs, dragged rafts over the rocks, and made portage around numerous river falls until they reached the settlement of Vancouver. Here they turned and began the upstream journey in the Willamette River, finally coming to Champoeg, where they left the waterway to make their way across the valley to the mission.

On the first day of December they sighted the buildings in which they were to remain for the winter. They had traveled in drenching rain for twenty days. The end of the trail, which should have brought cheers of delight, was observed in silence.

"Oh how we could have enjoyed our hospitable shelter if we could have looked around the family circle and beheld the bright faces that accompanied us on our toilsome journey almost to the end. Alas, they were not there," Lindsay wrote in the journal in which he carefully recorded the events of the wagon trek west.

During the next two and one-half years the Applegate brothers established their farms, and talked with others who saw the need for an emigrant route easier and less dangerous than that of the Snake and Columbia Rivers.

The dispute with Great Britain over the boundary of the Oregon Territory was not yet settled, and the men realized that in case of war the transportation of troops or emigrants this way would be difficult. A southern route must be found.

To the south the country was marked "unexplored" on the maps. Hudson Bay trappers who had been through that area said the mountains were densely forested and steep. The valleys were lush and fertile but "infected" with fierce and warlike savages who would attack, steal, waylay and murder. To the east were vast areas of parched desert wasteland.

"Open a wagon trail?" the grizzled trappers said. "Preposterous."

And so with a complete lack of encouragement, the party of fifteen men, who would blaze the Applegate Trail via southern Oregon and Nevada to Fort Hall, Idaho, and open a new wagon route into the Willamette Valley, departed from their families in June of 1846. They were gone for more than four months.

Jesse Applegate was named captain of the group. With him were Lindsay Applegate, Levi Scott, John Jones, John Owens, Henry Boygus, William Sportsman, Samuel Goodhue, Robert Smith, Mose Harris, John Scott, William Parker, David Goff, Benjamin Burch and Benit Osburn. Each man had a pack horse and a saddle horse to guard and care for.

Leaving from LaCreole (where Dallas now stands), the trailblazers moved south down the valley and camped the first night on Mary's River (near the current location of Corvallis). Continuing through the foothills of the Calapooyas, they entered a little valley where Indians were digging camas roots. Using sign language the travelers managed to explain to a wrinkled old Indian that they sought a route south.

He showed them a foot path marked by twisted brush tops that led through a prairie to the base of the main Calapooya mountain chain. That night the men stopped by a little stream in a peaceful valley. The grass was good and the ground was covered with sweet, red strawberries, Lindsay wrote in his journal. It was the country of their dreams.

For the next four days they moved through grassy, oak studded hills and narrow valleys. They crossed the Umpqua River and entered the Umpqua canyon with more than a little forboding. The narrow trail led through a gorge for four or five miles. Brush and fallen timber obscured the sides and dense thickets afforded the perfect opportunity for ambush. Lindsay picked up a number of broken and shattered arrows and the explorers knew that a large party of Indians had passed over the trail only a few days before.

On June 26 they divided forces, some exploring the canyon and others staying to guard the camp. The news was good. "We can get wagons through the canyon," the scouts said.

As they prepared to break camp the next day, the men found signs that Indians had surrounded them during the night. After an early start, they moved cautiously. "Whenever the trail approached thickets, we dismounted and led our horses and held our guns in hand, ready at any moment to defend our lives," Lindsay wrote. They had agreed never to be the aggressor.

The route led through broken country and sharp hills. The men pushed on.

Somewhat before they reached the Rogue River, Jesse spotted Indians posted along the mountainside. They stayed just ahead of the party, watching. When the explorers came to a meadow on the banks of the river, Jesse called a halt and said they would camp.

With the Indians, who at this point appeared to be no more than curious, lurking in the underbrush, camp was made near the center of the open space. The horses were picketed in the form of a hollow square. The men knew if the animals were lost, defeat in battle was their fate. They kept vigilant guard during the night. In the morning they could see the Indians occupying the same positions as they had when darkness fell.

Heavy dew had dampened the firearms, so after an early breakfast the guns were fired and reloaded, and the party moved on in two divisions, with the pack horses behind.

The Indians watched as the men crossed the Rogue River. The front division fell behind the pack horses and drove them across the river while the rear division faced the brush with guns in hand. The front division then turned and the rear division crossed under their protection. The river was deep and rapid and some of the smaller animals had to swim.

After the crossing the Indians came out of the thickets and tried to provoke the men. With some mounted and others on foot, they followed on the opposite bank of the river. Signal fires on the mountains preceded the explorers, but the Indians kept their distance.

The first glimpse of the Rogue River Valley came from a low ridge of hills.

Lindsay wrote: "It seemed like a great meadow interspersed with oaks which appeared like vast orchards. All day long we traveled over rich, black soil covered with rank grass, clover and peavine, and that night we camped on a stream (now known as Emigrant Creek) near the foot of the Siskiyou mountains."

From this point the course was to be eastward, through an unexplored region several hundred miles long.

The mountain climb started the next day, the men moving through heavy forests of pine, fir and cedar. There was no evidence of Indians but the constant vigil was not relaxed.

For the next five days they climbed. Around noon on July 4 they reached the summit of the Cascade range and came into a glade that had water and grass. From that they could see the Klamath River.

Moving through forests of yellow pine, they suddenly came in full view of the vast Klamath country.

"It reached as far as the eye could see. It was an exciting moment after the many days spent in the forests and among the mountains and the whole party broke forth into cheer after cheer," Lindsay wrote.

Now their progress was followed by columns of smoke rising in every direction. The Modoc Indian signal fire telegraph was operating.

On the shores of Klamath Lake the men found pieces of newspaper and other evidence of white people having been there before them. Camp was made on open ground so the Indians could not approach without being seen.

"We were but a handful of men surrounded by hundreds of savages armed with poisoned arrows, but with great care and vigilance we were able to pass through the country safely," Lindsay wrote.

Traveling along the lake shore for the next two days, the party reached a high, rocky ridge. The men decided to climb to the top to make observations. From this vantage point they sighted a large lake about twenty miles long. Beyond that and eastward was a timbered butte, the base of which appeared to be a low pass through the mountain range. They decided the best way to reach this pass was to circle the north end of the lake. They began the rocky descent.

It was rough going. Short lava ridges ran in every direction and between them were caves and crevices into which the animals might fall. The farther they went, the worse it became. They decided to retrace their steps. "This was easier said than done as we became separated among the rocks and it was some time before we could get our horses together again on open ground. When we did," Lindsay wrote, "we discovered that David Goff was missing. While in the lava field, he had discovered a band of mountain sheep, and in chasing them in hopes of fresh meat, he lost his way. We could not find him, so we decided to continue to the meadow country at the head of the lake by circling the lava beds, and there to camp until we could find our comrade."

As they started out, they spotted several canoes leaving the lake shore under the bluff, headed for what appeared to be an island in the lake. And then a welcome sight. A lone horseman riding along the shore approached the party. It was Goff. The Modocs had spotted him in the lava fields and supposing that a whole party was about to attack them from the rocks, they fled to their canoes.

After resting for several hours, the explorers started again toward the timbered butte. They had not gone more than a mile when they came upon a large stream (Lost River) coming into the lake. Nearly perpendicular banks made crossing seem impossible.

"Heading upstream we had not gone far when we discovered an Indian hiding under the bank," Lindsay wrote. "We surrounded him and made him come out, then by signs we indicated that we wanted to cross the river."

The frightened man led them for a mile or so and then pointed to a place where a huge rock spanned the river, the water passing underneath it with about ten inches on top. (This was the famous Stone Bridge on the Lost River, often mentioned by later travelers.) The men crossed the river, gave the Indian presents, shook hands with him, and left him standing on the bank.

APPLEGATE TRAIL

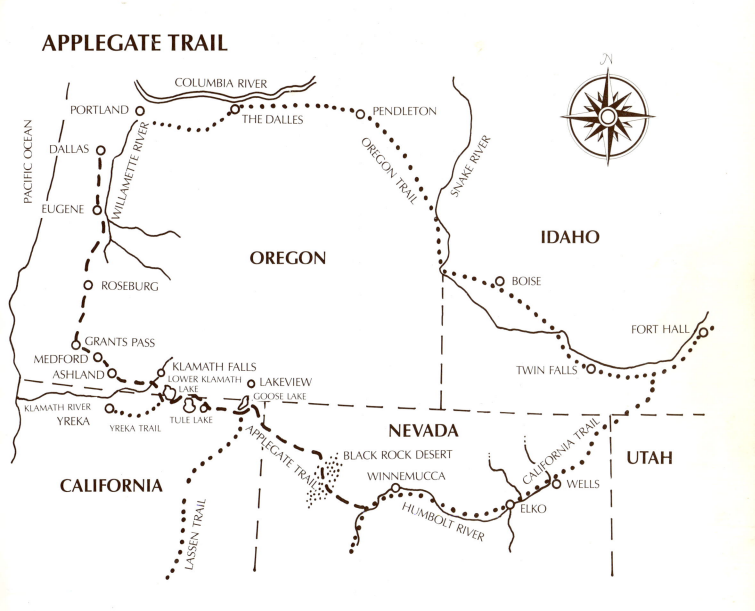

Camp that night was made near a fresh water spring at the base of the mountains. The fresh cold water was a luxury after the alkali water from the lower Klamath Lake they had used the previous night.

"There was plenty of dry wood and an abundance of green grass for the animals and we enjoyed the camp exceedingly," Lindsay wrote. "Sitting around the fire that evening we discussed the adventures of the last few days in this new and strange land. We talked of the vast fields of tule around the lake, and of the natural bridge, of the fact that the lake was an independent body of water, and of our desire to see more of this wild country."

The party left the valley of Tule Lake on July 7 and set their course eastward over a rocky tableland among scattered juniper trees. With the timbered butte as the landmark, they traveled as directly toward it as the country would permit. The landmark was passed on July 8, the party continuing eastward.

The country was quite level now, but rocky. The men passed the basin of a lake (Goose Lake) and crossed a valley about five miles long, then came to a grassy meadow.

Game was plentiful and one of the men killed a deer. The fresh meat and cool, clear water were a welcome treat. From a spur of the mountains near the camp they had a vista view of an extensive valley, the lake and the mountain range. The beautiful meadow country contained willows and a scattering of pine and cottonwood, indicating the course of many small streams.

"To the southeast of our camp there appeared to be a gap in the mountain wall and we decided to try for it on the next day," Lindsay wrote.

Captain Applegate moved his men up the ridge toward the gap where they entered a valley of several hundred acres, extending to the summit of the ridge. It would form an excellent pass and the ascent was gradual.

The valley was fringed with mountain mahogany trees that grew fifteen to twenty feet high. It was picturesque, giving the appearance of a cherry orchard, Lindsay wrote.

In the center of the valley a spring of cold water afforded a camping spot after what Lindsay described as "a long, tiresome march across the great American desert."

Standing on the crest of the ridge, the explorers surveyed the desert plains to the east, apparently without trees or grass and marked by high rocky ridges. They set their course, descended the mountain, and came to a stream, with banks that were lined with plum bushes loaded with fruit.

The rich valley held a grove of pine trees, and game seemed plentiful. While the explorers rested, a large band of antelope grazed within sight. After about two hours, during which time the trees filtered the blazing sun, the men packed up and moved eastward. These trees were the last they saw during their long dreary march across the desert.

"Small gravel made our progress laborious and by this time most of our horses were barefooted," Lindsay wrote.

They had despaired of finding water for the night when they came to a little spring. By digging they got just enough to wet the parched throats of men and horses.

"It kept us busy until midnight getting the horses all watered. Although we had met with singularly good fortune in finding water at the close of the first day's march on the desert, we could not always expect such good luck in the future, and so we lay down on our blankets among the sagebrush that night with gloomy thoughts in regard to the future of our expedition," Lindsay wrote.

Packing up on the morning of July 10, the travelers found the landscape before them anything but inviting. It was a vast sand plain, with no trees or mountains, broken only by dark ridges. The only vegetation was dwarf sage and greasewood growing in sand and gravel.

Under the hot afternoon sun, they came to a huge volcanic wall, varying in height from twenty to several hundred feet, that extended from horizon to horizon, from north to south. No gap was seen.

The men divided to explore both ways. After a few miles the party going south came to a stream that formed a meadow at the base of a wall and flowed through a narrow gateway into the ridge.

A rider was sent to overtake the second party with the good news. The men gathered in the meadow to feed and rest the horses and decided to explore the narrow defile on foot.

"We found it a very remarkable chasm extending nearly due east. The gateway was about sixty yards in width and the canyon was at some places a little wider than at others," Lindsay wrote.

It was wide enough for a wagon road.

Cliffs towered several hundred feet and overhung in many places. Signs showed this gateway was well known to the surefooted Indians.

The men returned to the meadow for the night and on the morning of July 11 they entered the gorge with their animals.

They reached the junction of a second canyon and a meadow of level ground, and in the afternoon they followed the bed of a dry stream that eventually led them to the east side of the ridge. Here they found a large basin but little water, and a great deal of mud. (The area later was named Mud Lake.)

The country eastward looked forbidding. Rising from a barren plain about fifteen miles away was a rough, rocky ridge that extended as far as could be seen toward the north, but apparently ended abruptly a few miles south. A few green spots along the base of the ridge indicated the presence of water.

"We considered the situation thoughtfully and concluded that the surest plan would be to leave the set course and travel southward to the extremity of the ridge, to keep away from the rocks and more probably find water," Lindsay wrote.

They followed the dry outlet of the lake about four miles where they made camp at a generous spring.

On July 12 towering columns of smoke or steam were sighted rising from the ridge. Traveling along the base of the ridge, the men passed several springs, some cold and others extremely hot. At the end of the ridge they found boiling springs with steam rising like smoke from a fire. The water was strong with alkali but was fit for use when cooled. Immense masses of volcanic rock formed the cliffs of the ridge and all about were huge piles of cinders. (The place now is known as Black Rock, one of the most noted landmarks in the Humboldt Desert.)

The adventurers rested a day and consulted as to the best way to reach the Humboldt River. They agreed to separate, one party to travel eastward and the other to follow a more southerly direction.

The next morning eight men headed south, and seven, including Lindsay, struck out toward the east.

The country resembled the dry bed of a lake. No vegetation could be found. Everything was white with alkali.

After going about fifteen miles, the men spotted rabbit trails, which became more visible and converged with many others, all pointing in the same general direction, toward a ledge of granite boulders.

Approaching the ledge, the first granite they had seen since leaving the Rogue River Valley, they saw a green mound where the rabbit trails centered. Here they found a small hole and a tiny puddle of water.

"This was a happy discovery for we were suffering from lack of water and our horses were nearly exhausted. The day had been terribly hot and the heat reflected from the shining beds of alkali in a most oppressive manner," Lindsay wrote.

The alkali water at Black Rock had given only temporary relief and the men's thirst was more intense from drinking it.

The horses were unpacked and staked in the bunch grass while the men began digging for the little vein of water. It was late at night before they got enough to quench their thirst. They named the spot Rabbit Springs.

Travel continued until the explorers sighted a vast desert plain, again without vegetation and covered with an alkaline effervescence that glittered beneath the scorching sun.

The heat was intense as they rode eastward. They headed toward what they thought was a large lake on the great plain. It was an optical illusion. Next they headed toward what appeared to be a clump of willows. Upon reaching the place, they found only a pile of black volcanic rock.

The only camp duty that night was to spread blankets upon the loose sand with little hope for rest. Without water, their thirst was nearly unbearable because of the alkali water they had drunk that morning.

"Even if we could have heard the cry of a night bird or the familiar note of the coyote, it would have given us encouragement for it would have indicated the presence of water. But not a sound was heard during the long night except our own voices and the restless tramp of our half famished horses," Lindsay wrote.

Starting the weary trek in the morning, the men could not see far ahead. Dense smoke enveloped the country. Much of the day they searched for water, finally stopping in the afternoon to rest in the shade of some rock ledges. Some of the men were too exhausted to ride, but were somewhat encouraged when they sighted a green spot that appeared to be about five miles away.

Robert Smith had physically fared the worst. He could not ride on and begged the others to leave him to rest a while longer under the cliffs. He would follow when he felt able.

With fears for his safety, but following the unwritten rules established by explorers, the men departed, leaving Smith behind. He was made as comfortable as possible before the men rode on.

After approximately a four-mile ride, a lone horseman came into view. It was John Jones, one of the party that had separated from them at Black Rock. Jones had found water at the place the men had seen and he was searching for the rest of his party when he found the weary group.

"We of course made a stampede for the water and upon arrival two of the party filled a large horn with water and started back to get Smith," Lindsay wrote. "On the way they met him staggering along, holding on to his saddle horn for support."

The two parties reunited at the water hole. The others had fared badly also and had not had water since the previous morning.

Although lifesaving, the water was almost as bad as could be imagined — about four inches of strong alkali water on a bed of mud in a lake thickly studded with reeds. It was so warm and nauseating that it was impossible for the men to keep a stomachful for long.

The horses drank and grazed all night on reeds and grasses.

Striking southeast the next day, the party came to immense peat bogs that were on fire. The fires extended for miles along the valley of the Humboldt River, for they were now near that stream, and at noon they reached the banks of the waterway. The river was sluggish and the water so strong with alkaline it had a milky hue.

Willows on the banks were used as fuel and bunch grass was available for the horses. "The camp was a good one," an encouraged Lindsay wrote. "Since leaving Rabbit Hole Springs we had traveled much too far south to satisfy us and our desire now was to move up the Humboldt until we could reach a point nearly east of Black Rock and find a route for our road in a more direct line on our course."

On July 19 the men headed northeast along the river bed. Travel was fairly easy and at noon on July 21 they reached a point where they could see what appeared to be a low pass through the ridge on the west, through which ran the channel of a tributary to the Humboldt River.

The men decided to camp and send out a party to explore the country towards Black Rock. They had nothing in which to carry water but a powder horn so they sent only Levi Smith and William Parker.

The two followed the stream bed for about fifteen miles and came to a spring of pure water. They spent the night there, and the following day they reached a grassy plain from which they could see Black Rock. Upon further exploration they found Rabbit Hole Springs.

Upon their return to the base camp, the entire company rejoiced.

"The line of our road was now completed. We had succeeded in finding a route across the desert and on to the Oregon Settlements, with camping places at suitable distances, and since we knew the course of the Humboldt River was near Fort Hall, we felt that our enterprise was nearly a success and that immigrants would be able to reach Oregon late in the season with far less danger of being snowed in than on the California route down the Humboldt and over the Sierras," an elated Lindsay wrote.

The men turned their steps homeward where they arrived on October 3, 1846. A party was sent with oxen and horses to meet the next emigrant train at Fort Hall and to help them reach the Willamette settlements via The Applegate Trail.

"For this assistance we made no demands," Lindsay concluded. "The consciousness of having opened up a better and safer road than that by way of the Columbia River was satisfaction and compensation enough for us for all our hardships and labors."

At the base of the Green Springs Mountain the Applegate Trail veered east, as does Oregon 66, the third replacement of the emigrant road.

A section of the grade of the original trail can be seen on the downhill side of Oregon 66 between Mileposts 14 and 15, an iron post marks the Keene Creek crossing near Milepost 16, and an historical sign board describes the path of the trail near Tubb Springs.

Tubb Springs, a state park on Oregon 66, is nineteen miles from Ashland and a great place to go for a cool-of-the-evening picnic on a hot summer day.

Lindsay Applegate.

BEAR CREEK

Bear Creek and Table Rock

Settlers called the main stream through the valley Bear Creek, ca. 1885.

BEAR CREEK

Bear Creek was known as Stuart Creek to the early settlers of this valley, named as a memorial to Captain Jimmy Stuart of the Oregon Mounted Rifles. Captain Stuart was felled by an arrow not far from Table Rock in June of 1851, the first soldier to be killed in Indian warfare west of the Cascades. His men buried him under a tree that came to be known as the Stuart Oak. Former Oregon Territorial Governor Joseph Lane proclaimed him the "bravest of the brave," all Oregon pledged his name would be remembered, and the settlers he died defending named the main stream through their valley Stuart Creek in his memory.

Within two years, however, the stream was being called Bear Creek. Bears were plentiful in the foothills it drained and meat meant food to the hungry men in the mining camp of Jacksonville. Records were sketchy, popular references were accepted, and when maps were drawn, Stuart Creek was recorded as Bear Creek. Eventually even the memorial oak fell, taking with it the captain's only epitaph, the initials J.S. carved deep in its bark.

Two years after Stuart's death a West Point classmate, George Brinton McClellan, later to be general-in-chief, was assigned to Oregon for military duty. He sought out his friend's grave and being a man who believed in records, he wrote:

"On the eighteenth of June, 1851, at five in the afternoon, died Jimmy Stuart, my best and oldest friend. He was mortally wounded the day before by an arrow whilst gallantly leading a charge against a party of hostile Indians. He is buried at Camp Stuart, about twenty-five miles south of the Rogue River near the main road and not far from the base of the Ciskiou Mountains. His grave is between two oaks, on the left side of the road going south, with J.S. cut in the bark of the larger of the two oaks."

A little more about the career of Captain Jimmy Stuart.

The regiment known as the Oregon Mounted Rifles was authorized by Congress in 1846 in response to urgent pleas from Oregon settlers. Jimmy Stuart joined at Fort Leavenworth. Because of the war with Mexico, however, the Oregon frontier was for a time forgotten and the Rifles were sent south into action. Stuart won two battlefield promotions, he was first over the wall at Chapultepec, and he returned to Fort Leavenworth unharmed.

In May of 1849 the Rifles left for the West, 600 men, thirty-one commissioned officers, 160 wagons, 1,200 mules and 700 horses strong. The regiment reached The Dalles in mid-October, then proceeded down the Columbia River to Fort Vancouver. As no quarters were available there, temporary billeting was assigned in Oregon City, but the townspeople objected. They had managed for three years with volunteer defense and they looked upon the Rifles as an expense and a disturbance in a temperate community.

Governor Lane, who had seen the Rifles under fire in Mexico and knew their worth, and his successor, Governor John Gaines, assured the men that regular army troops were welcome and needed, but others disagreed. Time passed and the controversy continued. Finally the Rifles were ordered to return to Leavenworth by way of Fort Benicia in California.

That is how Captain Jimmy Stuart came to be in Southern Oregon.

Riding south under Major Philip Kearney's command, the detachment had orders to map out a road through the Umpqua River canyon. Near Yoncalla they were met by Jesse Applegate who brought them the news of an Indian uprising in the Rogue River Valley. Applegate said volunteers could not handle the problem and he asked for help.

Major Kearney was faced with a decision. He was under orders to map a road, not fight a war. He singled out a few men to act as a scouting party and he put Captain Stuart in charge.

On June 17, 1851, the scouting party started out at daylight. The soldiers encountered Indians, but the conflict was short. Captain Stuart went down. His men got him back to camp but they could not remove the arrow that pierced his body. He lived through the day and part of the next, cursing the fate that allowed him to survive the hottest gunfire in Mexico only to die in the Rogue River Valley the victim of an Indian arrow.

Some historians say Stuart's grave was near the Colver house at Phoenix, but others claim it was closer to what is now Central Point. No photographs or drawings of the Stuart Oak are known to exist.

BEAR CREEK GREENWAY

The Bear Creek Greenway, its parks and developing network of trails, was established to preserve the natural character of the land, to protect the wildlife, and eventually to provide a woodsy corridor through the valley along Bear Creek.

The Greenway extends thirty miles from Emigrant Lake to the Rogue River, and encompasses parts of Ashland Creek, Little Butte Creek and the Rogue River.

You can enjoy parks at Emigrant Lake, Talent, Medford and Central Point. Others will be developed in the future. As of 1985, trails have been built between north of Ashland and Talent, from Talent toward Phoenix, and from Barnett Road, Medford, north to Biddle Road.

A walk or bicycle ride along a Greenway trail is delightful at any time of the year. Horseback riding is permitted except where the trail lies within the City of Medford.

A family enjoys the Bear Creek Greenway.

33

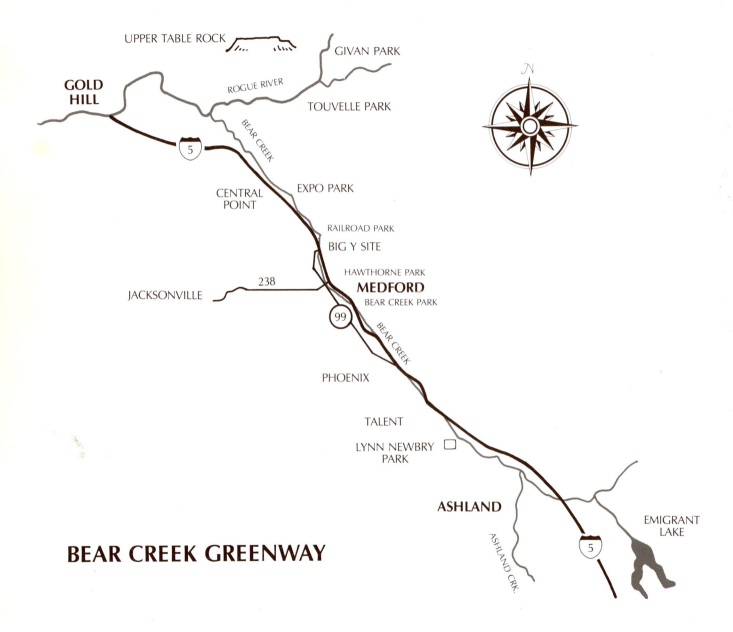

UPPER TABLE ROCK

GIVAN PARK

GOLD HILL

ROGUE RIVER

TOUVELLE PARK

BEAR CREEK

5

CENTRAL POINT

EXPO PARK

RAILROAD PARK

BIG Y SITE

HAWTHORNE PARK

JACKSONVILLE   238   **MEDFORD**

BEAR CREEK PARK

99

BEAR CREEK

PHOENIX

TALENT

LYNN NEWBRY PARK

ASHLAND

EMIGRANT LAKE

ASHLAND CRK.

5

BEAR CREEK GREENWAY

34

NOTES

MARYUM'S ROSE

24
CEMETERY
LOCTOWN ROSE
PLANTED HERE IN
1863 AND 1958

Maryum's yellow rose blooms late in May.

MARYUM'S ROSE

Maryum McKee was a bride in 1851 when she and her husband, John, left Missouri to join a group of settlers headed for the Oregon country. Traveling by ox-team and covered wagon, Maryum and her step-mother, Roxy Ann Bowen, were allowed to bring few treasures, few items of comfort or beauty for their new homes. They did bring one cherished possession, a yellow rose bush.

The wagon train was headed north for the Willamette Valley but the several McKee wagons (John's brothers, Joe and Dave, were in the group) and the Bowens left the main train and made their way south along the Applegate Trail across parched desert land and through the Klamath Lake country.

Gentle hands cared for the small rose bush.

The newcomers arrived in the Rogue River Valley during a time of Indian uprisings and they took refuge in a fort near what was to become Phoenix. When they could decide where they would live, they chose to homestead land lying at the foot of a predominate valley butte, a butte now known as Roxy Ann. Here Roxy Ann and Maryum planted the yellow rose.

The following year John McKee traded his homestead for a team of mules and the McKees moved to a gold mining claim on Poorman's Creek six miles from Jacksonville. Maryum took cuttings from the rose.

McKee built a fine log house with a big veranda style porch. Because he loved to dance, one of the rooms was large enough to accommodate two squares of dancers. Friends and neighbors gathered for squares, quadrilles, schottisches, polkas and waltzes, for quilting bees and parties.

Maryum planted the yellow rose in a corner of her dooryard near the gate. Often the women who came to the parties returned to their homes with rose cuttings.

Maryum was a busy mother as she cared for her twelve children. She washed fleece, carded wool, spun yarn and knitted stockings. The washing was done by the stream after heated water and soap were poured into big wooden barrels. To scrub the clothes, the smaller children jumped up and down in the barrels.

Maryum ground flour and prepared venison, pork or bear meat in iron kettles hanging over the fireplace or in big Dutch ovens. She never forgot to tend her rose.

The McKee property had belonged to Frank Logg. A supply point on the pack trail between Jacksonville and Crescent City, the area became known as Logtown. It boomed and declined with the gold mines. At one time 250 white persons and 400 Chinese lived there, mining for gold in the streams and valleys. Logtown included houses, a blacksmith shop, livery stable, store, two meat markets, hotel, saloon, Chinese huts, and Maryum's rose.

In 1885 (approximate date) most of the business buildings in Logtown burned. Eventually the McKees moved to the Big Butte area to make their home. Maryum left her rose.

In 1909 a McKee grandchild bought a car, a handsome new Buick. Proud of his automobile, he insisted he drive his grandparents back to see the old home place. Maryum hesitated. Memories of her early home were dear. Finally she consented to make the trip.

When the car came to a stop in front of the old log house, a cow poked its head out a broken window. The roof had collapsed in spots. Walls had fallen in. All Maryum could say was, "Little did I think when I lived here that one day I would drive up in a shiny automobile."

She started to walk around the building and a sudden smile took the trace of tears from her eyes. There by the broken gate, in the dooryard, was the rose she and Roxy Ann had carried on the long trip west nearly sixty years before. The big rambling bush was covered with yellow blooms. "Look, my bush. It is still alive," Maryum cried.

40

Through the years relatives and friends of the pioneer McKee family kept Maryum's rose alive. In 1958 cuttings were planted in the Logtown Cemetery where Maryum and John and several of their children are buried. The rose still blooms each year, usually in time for Memorial Day.

LOGTOWN CEMETERY

Plan a short trip to Logtown Cemetery in late May or early June and chances are Maryum's yellow rose will be in the height of bloom.

To reach Logtown Cemetery, where tombstones tell stories dating back to the 1860s, follow Oregon 238 six miles west of Jacksonville. The cemetery and off-the-road space to park is on the left side of the highway.

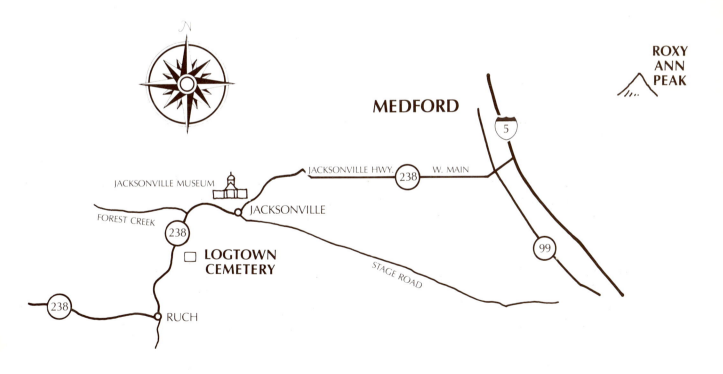

41

THE DUNN HOME

Patrick and Mary Dunn's descendants at the family home in 1952. Left to right, Robert Dunn, great-grandson, holds Michael Dunn, great-great grandson; Senator George Dunn, son of the pioneer couple; Edwin Dunn, their grandson.

THE DUNN HOME

In the spring of 1851 Patrick Dunn, a young Irish miner gaunt after a hard winter spent mining for gold in the Salmon River country of Northern California, crossed the Siskiyou Mountains, rested on the bank of a stream that cut through a grassy valley, and decided this was where his future lay.

For a time he mined near Jacksonville, then he returned to the stream where he built a log cabin and started to establish one of the first ranches in the southeastern part of the Rogue River Valley.

Only a few men lived in this part of the valley, and no women until Isaac Hill, who built a cabin and then went east for his family, returned in 1853 with his wife, Elizabeth, his daughters, Mary, Haseltine and Martha, and his son, Cicero.

The Hill family had known comfortable living in Tennessee and Elizabeth fought back tears when she first saw her wilderness home — a one-room log cabin with no windows, no furniture and a dirt floor.

"Our first summer was a busy one," Mary wrote in the journal she kept. "Mother nursed the sick, counseled those who needed care and sympathy, welcomed strangers and homeseekers and was often called upon to close the eyes of loved ones gone still further west."

The girls helped their father with the garden, milked cows, made butter and cheese for the packers headed over the Siskiyou Mountains, and did sewing and laundry for the Mountain House, a stop-over place on the trail south.

"Our few neighbors, all men, did not neglect their social duties," Mary wrote. "On Sunday morning we would awake to find the fence in front of our cabin lined with those who had come many miles to see The Hill Girls. Father would invite them in and we would cook a big dinner for them."

One of the regular visitors was Patrick Dunn.

And then for a time social life was put aside. Mary wrote of the struggle for existence.

"It was the first of August and the Indians began to act strangely. One day a big fellow came to the door of our home and began to sharpen a knife. He pushed his way inside, picked up a stool and threw it down, then walked across the cabin and jerked down the curtains that separated our beds. He spied father's gun and started for that. I sprang ahead of him, drew a gun on him and followed him as he backed toward the door."

At just this moment Patrick Dunn and a man named Gibbs, who had been following the Indian, arrived and took over. They decided that trouble was coming and the settlers should go to the Dunn place where they could be protected.

That night there was fighting and several men, including Patrick Dunn, were wounded. Several Indian men were killed and a group of Indian women and children were taken prisoners and brought to the Dunn place.

Before the hostilities ended, Mary and her sisters helped their mother "prepare seventeen Indian war heroes" for burial, and the Hill-Dunn Cemetery was established.

The Indians killed all of the stock on the Dunn ranch and burned the summer crop.

"All that was left was a few potatoes," Mary wrote, "but when the emigrant train came in (via the Applegate Trail) through the Klamath country, we shared what we had."

Then came winter and once again time for social life.

On February 23, 1854, Mary and Patrick Dunn were married, Haseltine married James H. Russell in May, and the following spring Martha married Alvin Gillette.

The wedding of Mary and Patrick Dunn was the first in Jackson County, which at that time included most of what is now Southern Oregon.

It was a big affair. The cook from the Mountain House spent three days preparing the feast. Isaac Hill killed a beef. Fruit and flour shipped from South America were packed inland from the port at Crescent City.

"Mr. Burns of Yreka baked a large fruit cake for the occasion and Aunt Kelly carried it in a bucket in her lap as she rode horseback over the Siskiyou Mountains," Mary wrote.

Guests came from as far away as Jacksonville and they brought gifts of cut glass and "kitchen things." Mr. and Mrs. Hill gave their daughter and her husband three cows.

"My dress was of thin white material much like fine Swiss," Mary wrote. "We had a rather large house by then with a big fireplace and we had a nice wedding. The Rev. Myram Stearns, a Baptist minister, married us at noon. We stayed that night at father's and went down to the Dunn house (two miles away) the next day. Here Mrs. Grubb, who kept house for Mr. Dunn, had prepared a big dinner to welcome me to my new home."

It is remembered that Mary always referred to her husband as "Mr. Dunn."

Mary's new home was a log cabin with unplaned floors, a few chairs, and a home-made table. A fireplace across the end of the room served for both heating and cooking.

"This was the beginning of a hard fight to make out of the valley a garden where church bells and school bells would soon be ringing, where the wildflowers so profuse would be replaced by waving grain, where apple, peach and pear trees would replace the mighty oak and fir," Mary wrote in later years.

Then came October 9, 1855, and word of an Indian massacre at the Harris home north of Jacksonville. (An historical marker at the Interstate 5 Manzanita rest stop, Milepost 62, north of Grants Pass, marks the site of the Harris cabin massacre.) Twenty persons were killed. Settlers living near Jacksonville went there for safety, others built "club houses" for protection. Those who lived east of Ashland went to the Dunn home.

"We covered the windows of our house with slabs and filled sacks with grain and lined the kitchen with them as high as our heads," Mary wrote. "We had portholes through which we could fire if we were attacked and we kept two barrels of water on hand in case we should be surrounded. Father and mother, the Alberdines, and others stayed with us. We lived this way all winter. The worst fighting was in the valley near Grants Pass. The next spring the Indians were subdued and sent to a reservation on the coast."

Patrick Dunn was elected to the first Oregon Territorial Legislature. On his return home from the first session he brought three dozen fruit trees and planted one of the first orchards in the valley. Along with ranch work, he served as Jackson County assessor, county commissioner and later county clerk. He was a prime mover in establishing the first school in the Neil Creek area.

With a box of Bibles, a Sunday School quarterly and several "singing books," Mary helped start a Sunday School.

"As the country was settled and business developed, we lived the life of any American family with varied interests of home, church and school," Mary recalled in later years. "During the Civil War we lived on what we could raise on our farms as nothing was brought into the valley. We did without coffee or sugar for two years. Carrots, cut and roasted, made a good drink, but were hard to prepare. News from the East was meager. I remember a letter mother received from her sister back there. 'Dear Besy: I have often remembered the morning you left the old place. I stood in the door and looked after you. I knew I would never see you no more till the judgment.' "

In 1860 the Dunn family had outgrown the log cabin, and the big two-story house that stands on Oregon 66 at the Neil Creek crossing east of Ashland was built.

"The home, just as our home had been in Tennessee, became the center of all kinds," Mary wrote. "We lived there until 1890 when we moved to Ashland and our son, George, took over the ranch." (Patrick and Mary reared three daughters and a son, George, who became an Oregon senator.)

Patrick Dunn died in Ashland on July 29, 1901, at the age of 77. Of him Mary wrote, "At last, completely worn out by the long struggle, the spirit of this old and rugged pioneer took flight and in the language of the text, 'In the evening there shall be light.' "

Mary Hill Dunn and her sister Haseltine Hill Russell at the Hill-Dunn Cemetery.

On June 23, 1927, Mary Hill Dunn was crowned Mother Oregon of the Oregon Pioneers and members of four generations of her family were present in Portland for the ceremony.

Mary lived to attend the seventieth gathering of the Hill-Dunn family, but when the one hundredth anniversary drew more than one hundred descendants to Ashland, she was not among them. She died in Portland at the age of 97 at the home of a daughter, Mrs. Ella Rice.

Senator George Dunn, who worked the ranch after his father, died in Ashland in 1961 at the age of 97. His son Edwin operated the Century Farm until his death in November of 1965. Edwin's son Robert still lives on part of the original ranch property.

The historic Dunn home was purchased in 1976 by Al and Margaret Meyer, who restored it and lived in it until 1984 when it was purchased by Dom and Joyce Provost of Ashland, who now make it their home.

EMIGRANT LAKE PARK

Emigrant Lake Park, in the narrowing end of the valley east of Ashland, is an ideal spot for an afternoon in the sun, for a family outing, or for a large group of good friends to get together for a relaxing and carefree day.

You will drive past the Dunn home enroute to the park, and if you wish, you may walk through the Hill-Dunn Cemetery, which dates back to the Indian Wars of the 1850s. The lake now covers the spot where the Isaac Hill's first log cabin home once stood.

Emigrant Lake Park is a full facility county park with boat launching ramps, swimming beaches, water slides, a playground, softball fields, picnic and overnight sites. It is three miles from Ashland by way of Oregon 66. The Dunn home, a private home listed on the National Register of Historic Homes, stands near the south end of the Neil Creek bridge.

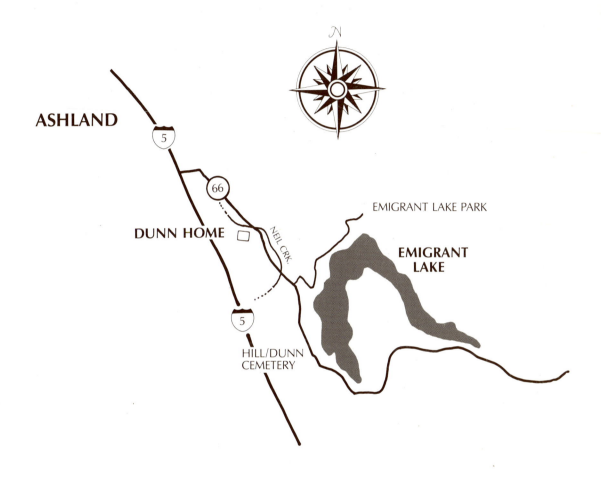

ASHLAND

5

66

DUNN HOME

NEIL CRK.

5

HILL/DUNN
CEMETERY

EMIGRANT LAKE PARK

**EMIGRANT
LAKE**

FORT LANE AND THE TABLE ROCKS

General Lane returning with his captive, Chief John.

FORT LANE

Fort Lane was built in 1853 after General Joseph Lane convinced the governor of the Oregon Territory there could be no lasting peace in the Rogue River Valley until a permanent military garrison was built here.

Joseph Lane, who had served as the first territorial governor of Oregon (1849-1850), knew the wild and reckless collection of trappers, hunters and miners who swarmed into the valley, and he knew the proud but savage Indians who believed they were being strangled by civilization. He knew a military force would be necessary to back up any peace treaty that might be made between the settlers and the Indians.

The Table Rock Treaty was signed in 1853 after two years of warfare, and the governor heeded Lane's advice. A military post was built on a grassy knoll overlooking the Rogue River and named Fort Lane. The fort also commanded a view of the two Table Rocks, the reservation where more than 300 Rogue River Indians were living, and the wide fertile valley to the south and east where white settlers were claiming farm land.

A high stockade enclosed the parade ground, barracks for the soldiers, houses for the officers, an armory, hospital and other buildings. All were built of logs.

When the troops arrived, they faced immediate problems. Several hundred Indians who had not accepted the terms of the peace treaty had followed their chief Tipsu Tyee into hiding, and the people the troops had come to protect had little if any faith in their protectors. The tough frontiersmen who had served in the volunteer forces during the Indian wars resented the snappy uniforms of the government troops. The frontiersmen had been unorganized, unpaid, poorly clothed and mounted on everything from plow horses to pack mules, but they knew how to fight Indians. They had no faith in the "fourth infantry, third artillery, first draggoons." They laughed because the army depended upon quartermaster and commissary trains. They said the army musketoon was a "firearm alike aggressive on both ends," and when they saw the cannon, the "mountain howitzer" the army brought from Fort Vancouver, they were sure the government troops knew less than nothing about Indian warfare.

The army men set out to prove their worth. They escorted emigrant wagon trains across the passes and they continued to explore the country, hoping to find a better freight route — to replace the packers' trail — between the Rogue River and the coast. When James Kyle was murdered two miles from the fort, they saw to it that the murderers were duly surrendered, tried and hanged. They rode after Tipsu Tyee, who was terrorizing settlers in a tract of country from the Klamath Lakes to the Applegate, too often arriving only to bury the mutilated remains of Tipsu's victims.

For two years the troops at Fort Lane were occupied with routine matters, then came the horror-filled day in October of 1855 when the Indians went on a rampage beginning at the Harris home north of Jacksonville. White settlers, men, women and children, were killed as a bloody path was cut through the Rogue River Valley.

When news of the massacre reached the fort, a major took a detachment of twenty-five mounted men to survey the damage and bury the dead. Civilians formed the volunteer army again; 500 men, most of them under the age of twenty-four, signed the muster rolls after taking women and children to places of safety. The volunteers agreed to fight with the regulars as well as mutual jealousies would permit, and together from Fort Lane they planned their first campaign.

It was not successful.

After a day and a night in the field, orders were given for a "retrograde march." The regulars blamed the volunteers; volunteers blamed the regulars. The "partial defeat" was blamed on foul weather and the fact that the army commissariat was in chaos.

The Indians continued to pillage and Governor George L. Curry in a proclamation called for all-out war against the Indians and said, "In castigating the enemies, you will use your own discretion, provided you take no prisoners."

The first Meadows Campaign started from Fort Lane under the governor's direction. The soldiers pushed their mountain howitzer through underbrush and up and down rocky inclines as the army made its way down the river canyon. When the commanding officer found a place to cross the river, he ordered some of the men to build rafts to ferry the command. Those who were not so occupied whiled away the time prospecting for gold along the river's edge. It was then the Indians, who were hiding behind every other tree in the canyon, began to fire.

The captain shouted, "Form a line here. Where the devil are you running?"

The lieutenant shouted, "Break for the brush every man of you who doesn't want to get shot."

History recorded, "And the privates thought the latter advice the best and hid themselves in desperate haste."

All the while the mountain howitzer was being fired from the top of the hill.

When the Indian attack let up a bit, a "retrograde march" was ordered, the howitzer was loaded on a mule, and the army retired.

That winter the regulars enjoyed the seclusion and comfort of Fort Lane; in the spring, the commanding officer said no furloughs would be granted until every last Indian in Southern Oregon was killed. The second Meadows Campaign was launched, the army devoured twenty-five days rations in two weeks time, and little else was accomplished.

Indian occupancy of Southern Oregon had reached its final days, however. "The soil whereon the red man had trod and from whence arose the smoke of his campfire was about to pass forever into the possession of an alien race," wrote historian A. G. Walling.

The Indians were hemmed in on all sides. They were without resources, without friends. They relinquished their land with one final struggle at Big Meadows. The last battle of the war was the most severe, and the regulars gave the volunteers due credit for its success by saying, "The part the volunteers took in termination of the hostilities was creditable."

The Indians were taken to a reservation at Fort Orford, the mountain howitzer was returned to Fort Vancouver, and Fort Lane was abandoned. A stone monument is all that remains to mark the place it once stood.

FORT LANE AND THE TABLE ROCKS

A short trip to the grassy, oak-studded knoll where Fort Lane once stood should be followed by a visit to the marker at the place where the Table Rock Treaty was signed in 1853, and, if you are in the mood for a bit of leg stretching, by a hike to the top of one of the Table Rocks.

Early spring is wildflower time in this area. The Table Rock trails are well designed and maintained and not too difficult, and the view from the tops is magnificent. Plan a full day and take a sack lunch if you decide to see it all.

To reach Fort Lane, follow Interstate 5 north from Medford to the Blackwell Hill Road interchange, Exit 35. Turn right on Blackwell Hill Road and follow it to Gold Ray Road just past the railroad overpass. Turn right on Gold Ray Road and continue almost a mile. You will see the Fort Lane monument on a hillside to the left.

To visit the Table Rock Treaty monument and climb the rocks, follow Table Rock Road from Medford past the Rogue River and Touvelle Park.

If you wish to hike on Upper Table Rock, turn right on Modoc Road and continue for a mile or until you see a power substation on the right and the trailhead on the left.

To reach Lower Table Rock, stay on Table Rock Road until you come to Wheeler Road, then turn left. The turnoff is well marked. The treaty marker is on the right side of Table Rock Road just after the road makes a sharp right turn before Wheeler Road.

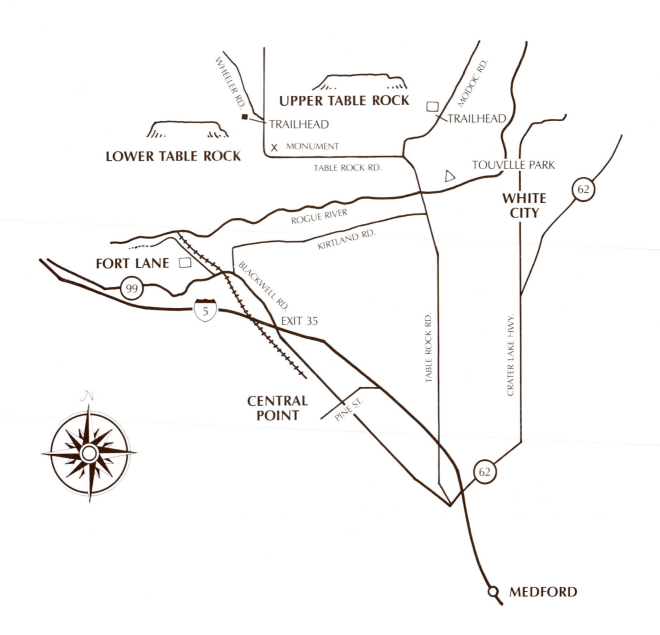

UPPER TABLE ROCK

TRAILHEAD

TRAILHEAD

WHEELER RD.

MODOC RD.

X MONUMENT

LOWER TABLE ROCK

TABLE ROCK RD.

TOUVELLE PARK

WHITE CITY

62

ROGUE RIVER

KIRTLAND RD.

FORT LANE

99

BLACKWELL RD.

5

EXIT 35

TABLE ROCK RD.

CRATER LAKE HWY.

CENTRAL POINT

PINE ST.

N

62

MEDFORD

THE COLVER HOME

The Colver home was a community center, ca. 1915.

THE COLVER HOME

Sam and Huldah Colver, pioneers of 1851, came west over the Old Oregon Trail. They took up a donation land claim on the banks of Bear Creek on a section of land they considered the most picturesque in the entire valley and started to build a house.

The house was huge because Sam Colver, known to the people of the valley as Uncle Sam, was a well-to-do, hospitable and public spirited man who envisioned his home as a community center.

And that is what it became.

The second floor, which later was divided into thirteen rooms, was a big, open hall used for a schoolroom, dance hall, church and lodge. Traveling ministers were invited to speak there because Mrs. Colver, who was known as Aunt Huldah, was very religious, even though Uncle Sam was an agnostic. Lecturers brought current and important information about temperance and other highly controversial issues of the day.

Abigail Scott Duniway brought her crusade for women's suffrage to this safe place after she was egged and burned in effigy in Jacksonville.

Historians say Sam Colver was ". . . an abolitionist, an advocate of women's rights, a prohibitionist of the most pronounced type, and a good debator always ready to express his opinion on any subject." He was one of the first to move toward forming a Republican Party in Oregon. He was the local Indian agent, and one of the signers of the Table Rock Treaty of 1853.

Aunt Huldah was a generous, kind-hearted woman who loved her flower gardens — she planted lilacs and many roses around the house — and her home. The Colver home was on the main wagon road through the valley and always open to strangers.

Uncle Sam enjoyed company, perhaps to provide an audience for the rhymes he loved to compose then recite or sing as he sat on the wide front porch after dinner. His ditties usually ridiculed some common frailty in human nature. It was these "rhyming witticisms and caustic criticisms" that caused him trouble when he was younger, trouble that early-day historians said brought about the "termination of his scholastic career" in Iowa. When he left college he went to Texas where he served as a Texas Ranger under Sam Houston (he fought in the battle of San Jacinto which established the independence of Texas) before he married Huldah and came west.

Sam Colver.

Huldah Colver.

Colver imported the first fine blooded horses and cattle into the Bear Creek Valley, bringing them from Canada. He ran pack and saddle trains to the gold mines in Eastern Oregon (now Idaho and Montana) and he purchased an interest in what was known as the Stearns ranch near Keno in the Klamath Basin country.

He took an active part in the Modoc Indian Wars. General Canby spent his last night at the Colver home in Phoenix before he went to make peace with the Modoc Indians and was killed.

Colver recognized the potential of opening up the Klamath country east of the Cascades, and volunteered to take charge of building a road over the Green Springs Mountain from Ashland. Under his direction nearly fifty miles of road (a predecessor of Oregon 66) were built for $600.

In 1884 Sam and Huldah Colver's only son, Louis, was accidentally shot and killed in Phoenix. The next year their daughter, Isabel Colver Rose, died of diphtheria. In 1891 Sam either drowned or froze to death while attempting to cross the ice of the Upper Klamath Lake on horseback. He was 77. Huldah died at home in 1907 at the age of 84. She was survived by seven grandchildren, including Lloyd Colver, son of Louis, who inherited the house.

After being occupied by the Colver family for nearly seventy years, the home was sold in 1923 to Edith Prettyman, who opened it as an inn, The Blue Flower Lodge, offering travelers home cooked meals and comfortable rooms. Later it was purchased by Mr. and Mrs. C. G. Peebler, who operated it as a dinner house until the food and gas rationing of World War II made this no longer possible. The Peeblers opened the house for a time as a museum and antique store. In recent years it has been a private residence.

A DRIVE THROUGH PHOENIX

The Colver house stands at 150 South Main Street in Phoenix — the southbound street through town — and is one of the oldest houses in Oregon.

Started in 1853 and completed in 1855, the house is built of logs fourteen inches thick secured with wooden pins. It is fifty feet square and two stories high. Phoenix was laid out around it in 1854.

The house is a private residence now, not open to the public, but it can be appreciated by walking or driving along South Main Street. And while you are in Phoenix, take time to visit the Stancliffe Museum. Staffed by volunteers and supported by donations, the Stancliffe Museum is in a small white house that stands just behind the city library and fire hall on Second Street.

THE STORY OF GASSY KATE

Miss Kate presides.

THE STORY OF GASSY KATE

The story of Gassy Kate and how Phoenix got its name, as told by O. A. Stearns, a settler of 1853, is taken verbatim from the book, "Early Days in Phoenix, Oregon," by Marjorie Neill Helms:

About the time of the outbreak of the Indian War, or just before, Sam Colver and John Davenport commenced to build a block house. They intended it to serve as a hotel and a store for general merchandise when completed, and also to serve as a rendezvous for settlers during the Indian troubles.

It was sometime during the early autumn of 1855 that the Indians, having met one quite serious defeat on the Rogue River, had scattered out and were attacking outlying and scattered settlements, that notices were sent out for all settlers to concentrate at best available points of protection, as nearly every able-bodied young man was in the various military organizations pursuing the campaign against the Indians leaving only men with families to hold the entire settlement against possible surprise attack.

Most all families within a radius of six miles gathered at the site of the block house then under construction, making quite a village of tents and wagons. Many of them engaged in the work on the block house at Lindlay's mill where they were sawing out timbers.

We remained there several weeks with many coming and going. Also, Mr. Waite had quite a force of men working on the mill, the sawmill being run night and day to furnish material for both mill and block house and several new industries which sprang up. There was quite a population.

In the evening after the day's work was over, there was usually a huge campfire burning in a central location and all the young people and many of the old used to gather around the fire, sing songs, dance and tell stories until bedtime.

Among all of this concourse, while there were quite a number of young men and bachelors, there was only one young marriageable woman. Her name was Kate Clayton, and she was employed by Mrs. Waite to help her cook for the men who were employed at the mill. She was a girl about twenty and one of the most fluent talkers I ever met.

As every young girl fourteen years of age and older was then considered a young lady, and usually had a dozen or more admirers, Miss Kate, from her position as almost sole attraction of that assembly, always had every available male congregate in her immediate neighborhood.

From her ability to carry on an animated conversation with a half a dozen or more admirers at once, as well as her prompt and witty repartee, she had been given the subrogate of Gassy Kate, the term "gassy" being a recent slang for "talkative," or as the dictionary would say, "light and frivolous conversation."

One evening soon after our arrival at camp the usual campfire company was gathered around the fire and Kate, as usual, was in the position of presiding Goddess, while gathered near her in rapt admiration were her numerous admirers, among them Hobart Taylor, Dave Geiger, Jimmie Hays, and a man named Black, who had a very decided lisp.

One of the men, during a lull in the talk, cast his eyes around the numerous gathering of tents and remarked, "I say, this is getting to be quite a town. We ought to give it a name."

"I think so too," said Black, "and I move we call it Hashville after Gassy Kate."

"Oh, no," said Hobart Taylor, "that sounds too small and insignificant. I move we call it Gassburg, that sounds more important."

"Second the motion for Gassburg," came from a dozen or more at once, and Gassburg it became from thence forward for more than twenty years.

Soon after the Indian War was over, a mail route was established between Portland and Sacramento. A post office was established in a small office across the road from the grist mill with S. M. Waite, postmaster, and he took his fire insurance plate "Phoenix" as the name for the post office. . . .

The village received no permanent increase as a result of the Indian scare, but soon after the war was over the discovery of gold in the Davenport diggins gave it a start.

NOTES

GRIZZLY PEAK

"The old grizzly came charging out of the brush . . ."

GRIZZLY PEAK

Folklorists like to remember Henry H. Chapman's story about how Grizzly Peak got its name:

We'd been fighting Indians most of the summer. It was 1855 and the Indians weren't a bit friendly to the idea of giving up their land to the white settlers.

Can't say that I blamed them much, but anyhow, we'd been fighting them and were ready for something a little more relaxing. Needed a little fresh meat and knew we'd better not waste any time getting it because the first snow of the season always hit the mountain peaks. That's where the grizzlies were.

We started out on a bear hunt. Along with me were the Wells brothers, Erastus, Joe, and the biggest one everyone called Frog. We made camp that night on a little stream that was near dried up, down at the bottom of the mountain.

Didn't sleep too well so we started up the mountain looking for bear while the morning fog still hung over the valley.

Joe was good at picking up track. He had the sharpest eyes you ever saw and before long he found a lot of tracks. He figured there must be five or six bear, and not too far ahead of us.

Well, we found them all right. Pushed through a thicket of buck brush and fir trees and there they were, running right up the mountain ahead of us.

We followed them until about noon, up and around the peak of the mountain to a big prairie where they separated.

Erastus said he'd go down the south side, Joe headed west, and Frog took the north direction. That left the east side for me.

I got out of the clearing and into the heavy brush again and began to feel a bit uneasy. The brush was over my head. I couldn't see the Wells boys, couldn't even hear them.

I worked my way around a rock to a little open space and there they were — two old grizzlies and four cubs, feeding on berries.

I had my double barrel muzzleloading shotgun packed with heavy buckshot, like we did for Indians, so I put an ounce ball on each load of shot and took aim. I let go at the closest bear and with the blast she fell. The others ran off into the brush.

Now this shot should have brought the Wells boys too — we had decided on this before we split up — but instead it brought something I wasn't at all ready for.

The other old grizzly came charging out of the brush, growling something fierce and running right at me. I loaded up quick and shot. She fell, rolled over a couple of times, got up and ran down the hill.

About this time I decided to reload my gun and get out of there. Then I heard her roar. She was coming right at me, that bear I'd shot and figured dropped dead in her tracks. Let me tell you that old grizzly was far from dead. Right then and there I got a heap of respect for that bear and didn't feel I could spare the time to stop and reload my gun.

I started running and yelling for the Wells boys. Glancing over my shoulder I saw the bear coming fast, about ten feet behind me. Across the clearing I saw Joe and Erastus break through the brush. I yelled to them that the bear was coming.

Just then she roared again and it scared the boys so bad they dropped their shotguns and ran. Erastus made for the brush and Joe climbed up a stump.

The bear was all but on me. I had powder and shot in my coat pocket but as I ran the coat flew back and the first swing that old grizzly made at me caught the coat pocket and tore it off.

I reached a big fir tree. The bear was right behind me.

I kept dodging around the tree, hoping Joe and Erastus would come to their senses, or that Frog would show up. The bear raked at me from one side and then from the other with those big claws. It was plain I couldn't last long there.

I yelled for the boys to help and made a dash for another tree but that old grizzly caught up with me. With one blow she hit me high, splitting my scalp to the bone from the top of my head to my eyebrows. I fell down and she was on me.

First she caught me by my right thigh, tearing the flesh from my bones. I struggled to get up. She caught me by the shoulder, ripped it apart. Then she went for my throat.

Those big white teeth sunk into my neck and tore out the veins, but somehow they missed the big one. If she'd got that one I'd have been a goner right then and there.

Blood was running in my eyes and I was near crazy. I shoved my hand into that big ugly mouth and down the bear's throat. She bit me through the wrist, caught my arm and bit into the hollow of my shoulder, and I guess I fainted.

In a mad fury she left me for dead and took out after Erastus and Joe.

Now each of the boys had a navy sixshooter tied over his shoulder with a buckskin string, but in the excitement they pulled the string knots so tight they couldn't get them undone.

Joe finally cut his string and got his gun loose. He yelled to Erastus to get out of the way, the bear was coming fast. As Erastus moved, the bear slashed out at his foot.

The boys were in a tight place — the bear looked to be the master of the field — but good luck turned the tide. Joe blasted loose and fired. The shot caught the grizzly in the neck and she was done for.

Just then Frog came plowing through the brush. I had opened my eyes and put my hand to my throat. When the boys came over I told them I was dying.

I think Erastus got sick, he turned his head away. Frog asked me how many bears there were and I told him fifteen or sixteen. The boys took off their neckerchiefs and bound them around my neck.

Erastus said we'd better get out of there because the bears would be back. Frog grabbed me up, threw me over his shoulder, and started to run, calling to Joe to bring the guns.

We jogged downhill and I heard Joe say he thought I was dead. Frog put me down, face to the ground. I'd just fainted, I guess, and the shock of the cold ground brought me around.

Frog picked me up again but I couldn't take it. I told him to throw me in the brush, I was dying and wanted to be comfortable. It was then Erastus had a real bright thought. He said if I'd been going to bleed to death, I'd have done it already. Must be I was going to make it after all, so Frog headed on down toward camp.

I don't know what time it was when we got there, but Erastus went on for the horses and when he got back they took me in to the old man Wells. He sewed up the holes and the boys rode about twenty miles to Jacksonville to get the Doc.

It took me the better part of six weeks to get up and around again, and a year or more to get my strength back. Never did go bear hunting again, just too damn dangerous.

A HIGH COUNTRY DRIVE

An amazingly good system of back-country roads criss-crosses the mountains that encircle the Rogue River Valley. These roads make good places for Sunday drives, especially after the first rain of late summer settles the dust and washes the forests clean and fresh again.

The following trip takes you to the back side of Grizzly Peak — through the country where Henry Chapman and the Wells brothers went bear hunting — then to Howard Prairie Lake, Hyatt Lake, and home. Tuck a Bureau of Land Management map in your picnic basket for additional reference and use it if you are confused at an intersecting road. Flipping a coin will not help you make the correct choice.

You won't find any grizzly bears here now, but one thing to remember when you consider any mountain trip is that on occasion you may be required, quite suddenly, to share the road with a logging truck. For this reason Sunday drives are suggested. Fewer trucks are apt to be on the roads then, but foresters say even this is no absolute guarantee.

High country ranch.

Follow Dead Indian Road approximately seven miles from its junction with Oregon 66 east of Ashland to the Shale City Road intersection. Turn left on Shale City Road, a road that has been widened and surfaced with gravel. This takes you to the back side of Grizzly Peak, into the pine, fir and cedar country.

The road affords a spectacular view of a high country ranch — open fields, a stream, several weathered ranch buildings — with the blue ridges of the distant mountains, Mt. Shasta and Pilot Rock on the southern horizon.

In several places spur roads intersect from the left. Consult your drawn-to-scale BLM map; stay right on the main Shale City Road that follows the ridge. A few miles farther you look down into the Lake Creek country to the north, then you get a tremendous view of Mt. McLoughlin.

After you have followed this road for ten miles, you break out of the forest and find yourself back on paved Dead Indian Road.

At this point you can return to the valley — this makes it approximately a one-hour trip — or continue on.

Shortly after you've turned right on Dead Indian Road a sign on the left marks Buck Prairie Road. If you plan to continue your drive, take this road. This longer route home will take another two and one-half hours or so.

Buck Prairie Road (this is a cross-country ski course in the winter) is oil surfaced for the first two and one-half miles. Use your BLM map if you are confused where spur roads intersect.

The forest is inviting and again offers several good views of Mt. McLoughlin. There are three or four small natural meadows before the road brings you into the Howard Prairie Lake road not far from the resort.

From Howard Prairie Lake follow the paved road to Hyatt Lake. This water provides a stop-over for geese and other waterfowl using the Pacific flyway and it is a bonus for the trip if you come when you can see these magnificent birds resting in a cove, eating and bathing.

Just past the Hyatt Lake Resort area watch for the Pacific Crest Trail crossing. It is well marked and a walk into the forest is suggested.

This road connects Hyatt Lake with Oregon 66 about twenty miles from Ashland. This is how you get home.

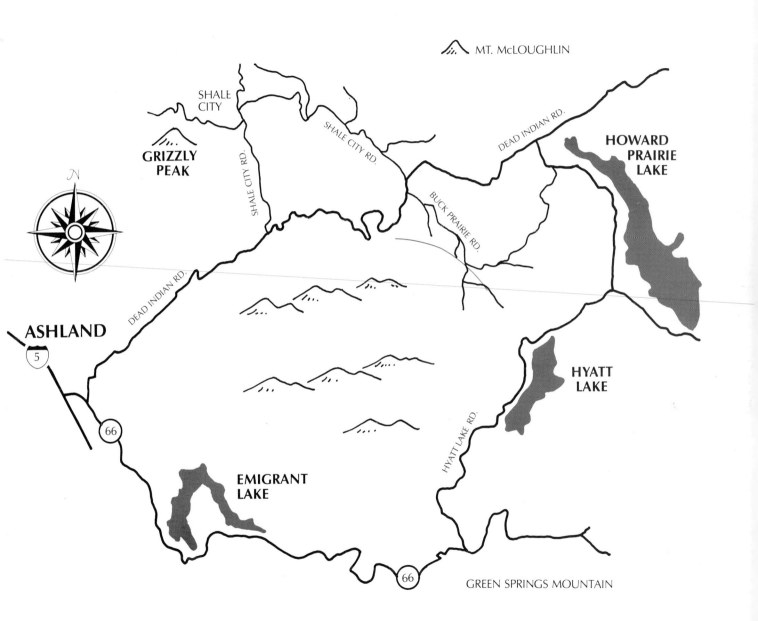

MT. McLOUGHLIN

SHALE CITY

GRIZZLY PEAK

SHALE CITY RD.

SHALE CITY RD.

DEAD INDIAN RD.

BUCK PRAIRIE RD.

HOWARD PRAIRIE LAKE

ASHLAND

5

DEAD INDIAN RD.

HYATT LAKE

HYATT LAKE RD.

66

EMIGRANT LAKE

66

GREEN SPRINGS MOUNTAIN

THE CHAVNER HOME

A chair for Father Blanchett.

THE CHAVNER HOME

AND A VERY SPECIAL CHAIR

Tom Chavner came to the United States from County Tipperary, Ireland, in the 1850s and headed west to seek his fortune in the gold fields. When he reached the Rogue River Valley, he decided this was the place he could make his dreams come true. He established a donation land claim, built a crude log cabin and began to work his land, both farming and mining.

One day Tom received word that Father Blanchett, the missionary priest who later became archbishop of Oregon, had been invited to visit this sparsely settled area that offered few if any physical comforts. He looked around his home at the crude furniture he had built to serve his own needs and decided that he would order a chair for the visiting dignitary.

Tom sent word to Boston that he wanted a rocking chair made by the finest craftsmen in the land. It was to be carved out of New England walnut, with grapes and leaves as the decorative pattern, and the cushion was to be stuffed with horsehair so it would be soft.

The chair was made to order and shipped west around the Horn to the port of Crescent City. From there it was brought by pack train to the Chavner cabin in time for Tom to receive Father Blanchett.

In due time life on the Rogue River homestead began to see changes. In 1860 Tom found the fortune he had been searching for, gold. The Gold Hill pocket was considered one of the richest strikes in the entire area. Margaret Brennan, who also had come from Ireland, became Mrs. Tom Chavner, and they had children, Michael, Peter, Anthony, Mary Ann and Margaret. The rocking chair ordered for the traveling priest became one of the most well-used pieces of furniture in the Chavner home.

When it became known that a railroad would be built through Southern Oregon, Tom laid out the townsite of Gold Hill and donated it as such so the railroad company would choose this place as a stop along the valley route. He built the first bridge across the Rogue River and part of the road later known as the old South Pacific Highway.

Many years passed. The rocking chair made for Father Blanchet was forgotten until one day in 1966 when Ruth Thompson, wife of Chavner Thompson, a grandson of the pioneer couple, explored one of the outbuildings on the family home property she and her husband shared with his mother, Margaret. She found the chair in which Margaret had been rocked as a child and decided it should be restored.

While the restoration work was under way, Ruth wrote a poem about the history of the chair and lettered it carefully on parchment. The last six lines read:

> "The family is smaller now as years have gone by,
>   Margaret, the only one left, carrying on without a sigh.
>   Ninety-four she is this year,
>   Still living on land her father pioneered.
>   Many pleasant memories are attached to this little chair,
>   As should be with all families who really care."

THE HOUSE IN THE TREES

The lovely old three-story Queen Anne style home Tom Chavner and his wife* built in 1891 stands in a grove of manzanita and oak trees just south of Gold Hill, on the left side of Blackwell Hill Road about two-tenths of a mile south of the Rogue River bridge. It is a private residence still in the family, not open to the public, but a long look from the roadside is permissible and worth the trip.

Three scenic routes from Gold Hill back to Medford offer three pleasant choices. You can follow Blackwell Hill Road south eight miles to Central Point, take Oregon 234 seven miles to Sams Valley and return via Table Rock Road, or follow Old Stage Road twelve miles through the foothills to Jacksonville.

*Rose McAndrews of Medford and Tom Chavner were married after the death of his first wife, Margaret Brennan.

The house Tom Chavner built.

THE BIRDSEYE HOME

Effie Birdseye was honored as Oregon's Unconquered Spirit.

THE BIRDSEYE HOME

1965: A VISIT WITH EFFIE BIRDSEYE

"They told me, 'Don't cry on our shoulders when you lose the place, Effie' and it made me so mad. They called me a 'mere woman' and said I couldn't pay off the farm alone. 'Set it up and sell it,' they said.

" 'This place belongs to me and my boys, and we are going to keep it,' I told them. 'I know what I can do, and I am going to do it,' and I did . . .

"But come in, we needn't stand here on the porch talking."

Effie Birdseye lived in the log house her father-in-law, David Nelson Birdseye, built for his bride, Clarissa Fleming, in 1856. The Birdseye donation land claim bordered the Rogue River and extended from mountain to mountain across fertile valley land just up-river from the present day community of Rogue River.

"The boys are going to modernize the kitchen for me, bring water in, but I just told them to leave the rest of the house as is," Effie said as we walked into the living room. She stooped to put a chunk of wood on the fire in the fireplace and there was no questioning the resolution so clear in her eyes when she added, "People need their memories."

Effie Birdseye moved into the house after her marriage to Wesley, one of the five children the pioneer Birdseyes reared on the farm.

"Wesley's father died before we were married," she said, "and everybody told me I couldn't live with his mother, but we lived here together until she died and we got along just fine."

The decision of what to do with the farm was left to Effie when her husband died. Alone, and with three young sons to provide for, she decided, against the advice of her counselors, to carry on, to buy the 360-acre property from the other heirs, just as she and her husband had planned to do.

"This is when I showed everybody what a 'mere woman' could do," she said.

With her son, Glenn, she milked a seventeen-cow dairy herd by hand morning and night, she sold milk and eggs, and in five years time she had saved the farm.

During Franklin D. Roosevelt's administration Effie Birdseye was honored as Oregon's Unconquered Spirit. She traveled to Pittsburgh to participate in the nation-wide program, but throughout all the excitement she just kept "looking back toward home."

It was impossible to sit in Mrs. Birdseye's parlor without looking around and asking questions.

"I've kept these things in here because I love and enjoy them," she said. "My mother-in-law used to say, 'Effie, why do you bring all that old junk in here?' but I just couldn't bear to see things like these stored out in the shed."

There stood a large copper kettle that came west on the wagon train that brought Clarissa Birdseye to the Oregon Territory. In a corner were Indian bowls and pestels picked up on the farm, Indian baskets, homemade farm rakes and a thrashing flail. The fireplace that had been used to warm the house for more than one hundred years had a high narrow mantle and above it hung a large mirror that had reflected images of the past as well as of the present, because Effie Birdseye insisted that no changes should be made.

The focal point in the room was the rosewood Chickering piano David Birdseye bought in 1866 for his 10-year-old daughter Addie. The piano was made in Boston, shipped around Cape Horn and brought by wagon from Crescent City to the Rogue River Valley.

Above the piano hung a Currier and Ives print that Clarissa Birdseye had framed by pasting bits of pine cone on a circle of cardboard. A graduate of a girls' finishing school in Virginia, the 18-year-old bride had done what she could to bring refinement to her home in the west.

This led to questions about Clarissa.

When she first came to the valley, she lived in Jacksonville, her daughter-in-law said, but she didn't like the rough mining camp. After she married David Birdseye, she insisted that she wanted to live on the farm. The log house was built and David and Clarissa moved in; David drove a horse and buggy to his store in Jacksonville every day.

Clarissa made friends with the Indians camped in the valley. They brought her venison, fish and camas root. She learned to talk with the Indians and she let them entertain her infant son Jim. She deplored the way the majority of the white settlers treated the Indians.

Clarissa had a reputation of having a mind of her own and a sharp tongue. "She ran off the hired girls who left kettles soaking on the stove," Effie remembered. "I never did that. We got along just fine."

The afternoon was gone — it was time to leave. Mrs. Birdseye's son, Glenn, who farmed the property and made his home with her, would soon be in for the evening meal. As we followed the path of flat stones that led from the porch past the grape arbor to the tree-bordered drive, Effie said, "This grapevine was started from a whip Clarissa cut from a vineyard in Jacksonville one day when she needed to hurry her horse home. When she got here, she stuck the switch in the ground and told her husband she was going to have an arbor, and she did.

"She always told me, 'Effie, if you want something, you are just going to have to stick with it until you get it. Don't let anybody tell you that you can't.' I guess I remembered that when they called me a 'mere woman.'"

Effie Birdseye was born in 1883 in Hillsboro, Oregon. She died in May of 1966 in Grants Pass.

HISTORIC HOME OPEN TO PUBLIC

The Birdseye home, built in 1856 on the banks of the Rogue River, is on the National Register of Historic Places and is open to the public between 2 and 4 p.m. the last Sunday of each month. Admission is $2.50 for adults, $1 for children. The house has been restored, is still occupied by members of the Birdseye family, and is the subject of the book, "Clarissa — Her Family and Her Home," written and published in 1984 by Nita Birdseye. The old-fashioned flower beds have been replanted.

Follow Interstate 5 north from Medford. At Exit 43, leave the freeway and follow the Rogue River Highway. The Birdseye home stands on the left side of the highway just past the Foots Creek Store.

If the day calls for a picnic, the Coyote Evans wayside is on the banks of the Rogue River two miles past the Birdseye home. Palmerton Park and arboretum is another beautiful place on the banks of Evans Creek in the community of Rogue River.

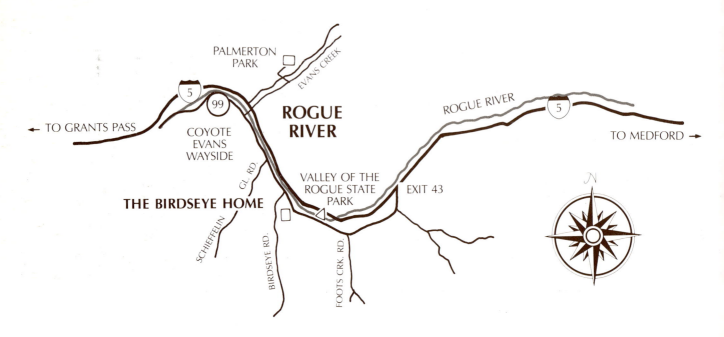

The Birdseye home.

FORT KLAMATH

The National Guard of Oregon, volunteer cavalry, signed up in Ashland for duty at Fort Klamath, ca. 1884.

FORT KLAMATH

Fort Klamath was known as one of the most beautiful frontier posts in America. The fort sprawled hospitably in a valley that was a wilderness of natural grass and lush pasture patterned into sections by six crystal clear streams that splashed down from the snow-covered Cascade mountains above. A low ridge of rimrocks held the valley securely at one end and at the other was the open vastness of Klamath Lake with Mt. Shasta faintly outlined on the distant horizon.

Fort Klamath was established during the Civil War and for the first seven years it was manned by a volunteer cavalry, men who signed up in the Rogue River Valley and trudged over the mountains singing, "I'm a raw recruit with a brand new suit, one hundred dollars bounty. I've just come down from Ashland town to fight for Jackson County."

It served for thirty years and when it was abandoned, the valley returned to its pristine glory.

Today a monument marks the site of the old fort — the 1,050 acres that were military reserve and the 3,135 acres the government set aside as a hay reserve. If you stop here and let your imagination drift back into time, you can almost join David Linn as he stood near the spot where Fort Creek joins Squaw Creek and decided how he would lay out a military installation.

In 1861 David Linn, a Jacksonville carpenter, contracted with the government to build a garrison to be known as Fort Klamath. The post was needed, government officials said, to protect the frontier from Indians and from "internal strife" during the early days of the Civil War. It was to be manned by volunteers because the regulars were on the eastern battlefields.

A primitive sawmill was located on Fort Creek and with lumber cut in it Linn built quarters for officers, an adjutant's office, a guard house, arsenal, store house, small hospital, bakery, barracks and stables. The stables were said to be the best buildings on the fort. The one hundred and twenty-five-foot flagpole erected on the parade ground served as a symbol of government and a center from which all surveying and measuring was done.

When the troops arrived, a ragged lot as each man furnished his own horse and equipment, they patrolled trails, acted as scouts and escorts, built roads and winter camps and attended to Indian problems as they came along.

Life was arduous, the men were lonely, isolation was a problem, reading material was limited. Because of this the volunteers started to publish a newspaper, a handwritten sheet they called The Growler. Fiction was accepted when news was lacking.

One issue of The Growler contained a particularly exciting plagarism of "The Last Days of Pompeii," recounting a tremendous earthquake at Fort Klamath, ". . . the tall pines lashing themselves into a fury, cattle moaning, unearthly yells of Klamath Indians. We imagined we were amid the wreck of matter and the crush of worlds, and were of the opinion a volcano had broken loose under the Klamath Marsh."

This particular issue of The Growler was sent to the Rogue Valley to be set in type in Jacksonville, and somehow the story reached the telegraph wires — and the world. The joke was not easily explained. The writer was given the protection of anonymity.

In July of 1867 the U.S. Cavalry rode into Fort Klamath and the volunteers were released to return to their homes in Jackson County. Two years later the men from the fort built a boat and launched it on Crater Lake, lacking, apparently, more important things to do. In 1870 more buildings were constructed at the fort.

The troops stationed at Fort Klamath were involved in the Modoc Indian War of the 1870s, and as a result the trial of the Modoc leader Captain Jack and his subchiefs, Schonchin John, Huka Jim and Boston Charley, was held at the post beginning on July 5, 1873. The Indian leaders were hanged in October and life at Fort Klamath returned to routine. The soldiers acted as military escort to the federal paymaster whose job it was to deliver pay, in coin, to Camp Warner, Camp Harney, Fort Bidwell and Fort Klamath. They built a telegraph line to Fort Bidwell (Northern California) and to Ashland.

In this post-Modoc War period, the fort became the social center for the southern region east of the Cascades. A little theatre was built and members of The Klamath Minstrels and the Linkville Amateur Variety Company were available to entertain. Songs, dances, and what historians record as "roaring farces" highlighted Washington's Birthday, the Fourth of July and other holidays. There was romance, too, when the young soldiers eloped to Ashland or Linkville (now Klamath Falls) with the settlers' daughters.

In 1880 the government began to talk of saving money by closing as many frontier posts as possible, and in 1886 President Grover Cleveland ordered Fort Klamath to be abandoned.

A furor arose. Civilians attended mass meetings and circulated petitions and letters of protest. Fort Klamath, the only remaining fort in Oregon, was saved until July 20, 1889, when the Secretary of War wrote the Secretary of Interior that "the time has come."

On August 9, 1889, the captain and staff stood at attention as the great flag of thirty-eight stars was lowered, a sign of abandonment of the post by the military. The captain received the carefully folded ensign and moved away. At his command the garrison moved out, the great freight wagons carrying what had not been buried or left behind. They headed for the Vancouver Barracks.

A few enlisted men were left to protect the property but during the following winter — the hardest winter recorded in that area — twenty feet of snow fell on the valley and many of the buildings collapsed. In June of 1890 the last detachment left the fort with only John Loosely, custodian, staying on. The days of Fort Klamath as a military post ended.

Settlers and ex-soldiers continued to return for holiday festivities. Indians joined them, participating in parades, feasting, dances and gambling. Oregonians believed for many years that the fort would be reconstituted as a military post, but nothing was done. In 1900 a movement to have the fort set aside as a front door to Crater Lake was started, but before the status of the tract could be ascertained, the buildings that remained were razed and moved.

Fort Klamath is gone. The story has been carefully recorded in the book "Fort Klamath," by Buena Cobb Stone, Klamath Falls historian, and the valley is still as beautiful as it was when it was the site of one of the most remote frontier posts in America.

A DAY FOR EXPLORING

A trip to Fort Klamath — through the Cascade mountains, skirting the Klamath Lakes, and finally across wide meadows of rich natural grass — is a trip for any season of the year when the day calls for exploring.

The Fort Klamath historical marker stands by the side of Oregon 62 south of the present day community of Fort Klamath, about where the flagpole once stood on the parade ground of the frontier fort.

It is approximately seventy miles from Medford to Fort Klamath via Oregon 140 and the paved and good secondary road that takes you along the western edge of the upper Klamath Lakes and the upper Klamath National Wildlife Refuge. (The Rocky Point intersection is well marked with a sign that directs you, Fort Klamath, 24 miles.) The Wood River campground is a good place for a picnic.

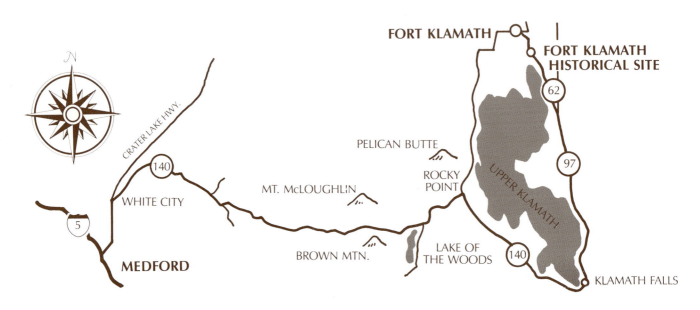

NOTES

BUTTE CREEK MILL

Peter Crandall dresses the millstones.

BUTTE CREEK MILL

Two millstones quarried in France and assembled in Illinois were shipped around Cape Horn to Crescent City in 1872, then carried by wagon train over the mountains and into the Rogue River Valley.

The big round, white stones weighed 1,400 pounds each and were put into service in a water-powered mill that John Daley Sr. and Eber Emery built on the banks of Little Butte Creek. They ground wheat into flour for the people of the new settlement of Eagle Point.

The millstones, also called buhrstones, still grind flour, and the power that turns them with a soft rhythmic sound still is water.

The floor boards in the sturdy old four-story mill throb gently as the big millstones turn, stirring up the tangy fragrance of wheat, rye and corn. Few changes have taken place in the appearance of the weathered building with the long wooden loading dock where grain wagons once waited to be unloaded. Lumber for the structure was cut from a pine stand near Butte Falls and hauled to Eagle Point by wagon. Some of the foundation pillars are sixteen inches square and were hewn in the woods with a broad ax, its marks still showing.

Stairs lead down to the lower level where water that has been diverted from the stream through a millrace activates a turbine that turns the wheels that supply power to the machinery. The water is then discharged back into the creek. When the mill was built, there was no electricity or gas power, so the power that turned and moved everything was water or gravity. Grain brought to the dock at ground level was carried to the upper level storage bins by belt-driven elevators — metal cups attached to a canvas belt. The miller then used gravity to feed the grain back down to the grinder on the floors below.

Peter and Cora Crandall came to the Rogue River Valley from Camarillo, California, in 1972 and bought the mill. Peter, a mechanical engineer for North American Rockwell Corporation, learned the skills of a miller from Frances Putnam Jr., whose family had operated the mill for some forty years.

The Crandalls recognize the importance of good nutrition. In the Butte Creek Mill Country Store you will find stone ground flour, meals, cereal, rolled grain mixes and a variety of other healthful foodstuff and snacks.

HISTORIC MILL OPEN

Butte Creek Mill is listed on the National Register of Historic Places. It is open 9 a.m. to 6 p.m. Mondays through Saturdays, except for major holidays, and owners Peter and Cora Crandall welcome visitors.

Eagle Point is ten miles from Medford via Oregon 62, the Crater Lake Highway. Attractions are a park on the banks of Little Butte Creek just downstream from the mill, a small city museum in an old school building, and a country store museum next door to the mill.

This is a good local history short trip, especially when you are looking for something special to entertain out-of-town visitors.

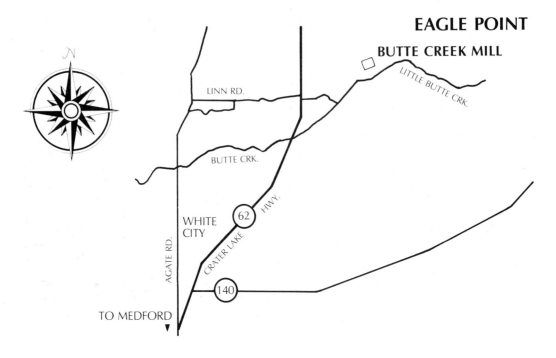

Butte Creek Mill.

CLIMAX

The Jacob Worlow home served as the Climax post office.

CLIMAX

It is like another world, remote from the Rogue River Valley and yet so close. Those who live there — the mountain country that stretches north and east from the back side of Grizzly Peak, across forested ridges and skyline meadows — call it "God's Country."

On the map it is marked with the word Climax, the name given the post office established in the 1880s to accommodate the twenty or more homesteads that formed a rambling sort of community.

Homesteaders chose this mountainous country for a number of reasons. "There was wild game, water, and plenty of rich, open range," Claus Charley, grandson of William Charley, one of the first settlers, once explained. "It didn't take much to live. Families would fence off a little garden patch then turn cattle, hogs and chickens loose to care for themselves."

Eventually the homesteads were abandoned. "I often wondered why," Charley said. "I guess the people left when it started to take more money to live, when better methods of transportation made it possible to come to the valley to work for wages, and then the country was fenced, making open range a thing of the past."

Antelope Road is the only road to Climax today, but in the early days another road meandered southwesterly down the face of Grizzly Peak into Ashland.

"It was over this eleven-mile road the homesteaders drove cattle to market, hauled farm produce, lumber, shakes and poles to the settlers below," Charley remembered. Four-horse teams pulled heavy laden wagons down the twenty-mile Antelope Creek route into Eagle Point and the "malaria area" — their name for the valley — where Medford was just a cluster of buildings along the railroad track.

One of the first houses in the Climax area was built on the Jacob Worlow homestead established in the 1870s — the house still stands, a private home — and it was here the Climax post office was established in 1891. Mail service was between Climax and Wellen, a way station out of Eagle Point, and delivery was three times a week. This service was discontinued in the early 1900s and for the next eight years the mail for Climax was carried by a horseback rider who rode from Ashland over the steep Grizzly Peak road, a ride that took a full day.

William Henry Holman brought his family from Iowa to Climax in 1891 and purchased what was known as the Bagley homestead. He ran a few cattle and made posts and shakes for a living. Others logged with oxen and operated small mills.

Charles and Minnie Applegate moved to a ranch in the Climax area in 1911. In later years Mrs. Applegate fondly remembered the dances that were held in their home, and how the neighbors danced through the night to violin music. Mrs. Applegate made butter, forty or more pounds each week, and took it and the chickens she raised into Ashland to market. She recalled the night she held the kerosene lamp while a doctor performed an emergency operation. "It didn't seem far to run to the neighbor's place when we were young," she said.

The children attended a country school, and the Fourth of July was an occasion that drew many people from the valley to celebrate with a picnic and visiting.

Memories grow dim and names begin to fade, but old-timers still talk about the Charleys, the Worlows, the Holman ranch, the Hansen place, the Orchard ranch, the Grissoms "who lived over the mountain," the Ed Whites, the Thompson place, the Moores, the Rummel family. Mrs. Lester Wertz maintains the home her parents, the Hansens, purchased from the Worleys.

As for the rest of the Climax area, a few fruit trees that have gone wild mark places where farm houses and buildings once clustered around mountain springs, but little else remains. "You can find these places clear back to Lake of the Woods," the old-timers will tell you. "They are most all abandoned now, fallen to ruin."

To drive to the Climax area, take Oregon 62 to the intersection of Oregon 140 at White City, follow Oregon 140 three and one-half miles to the Antelope Road intersection, turn right on Antelope Road and continue for another ten miles. There are no improved picnic areas, but a lunch stop under a tall oak tree at roadside can be delightful.

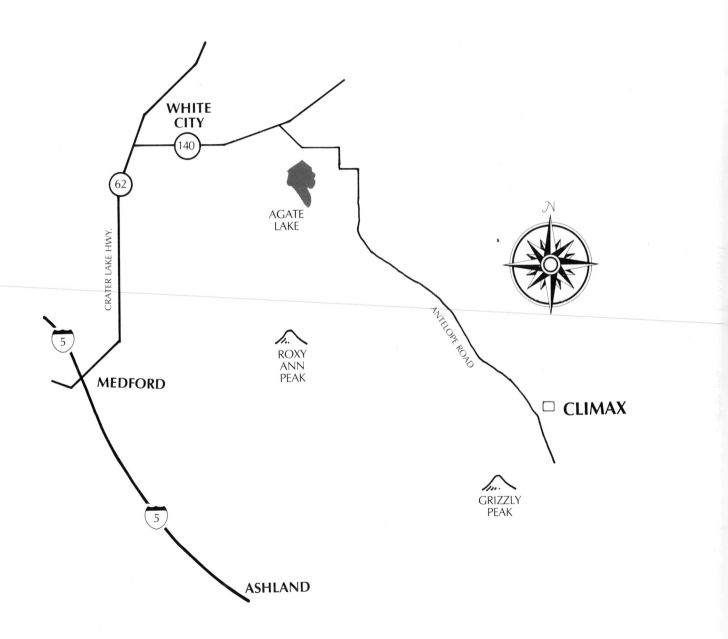

WHITE
CITY
140
62
CRATER LAKE HWY.

AGATE
LAKE

5

MEDFORD

ROXY
ANN
PEAK

ANTELOPE ROAD

CLIMAX

5

GRIZZLY
PEAK

ASHLAND

UNION CREEK

The road to Crater Lake, ca. 1909

UNION CREEK

The Union Creek Resort stands near the place where Union Creek flows into the turbulent upper Rogue River just below Rogue River Gorge. You can fish here and hunt for mushrooms in the spring, camp and hike in the summertime. The autumn color is beautiful and winter offers snow sports.

Union Creek is fifty-six miles north of Medford on Oregon 62, the Crater Lake Highway. During summer months the U.S. Forest Service (Prospect district) information office is open at Union Creek where you can obtain information concerning the trails, camps — more than 200 units in the district, including sixty at Union Creek and forty at Farewell Bend — and other recreational areas.

Union Creek lies in the transition area between the Ponderosa pine and Douglas fir zones. Sugar pine, white pine, Noble fir, white fir, lodgepole pine and western hemlock, all are found here. Both blacktail and mule deer make these forests their home, sharing with coyote and black bear.

The scenic beauty of this country is long remembered by visitors. Hiking trails are well marked. A walk to the natural bridge and Rogue River Gorge, both near the resort, is nature's invitation to view wild splendor.

Union Creek Resort — Becky's Cafe, the lodge, housekeeping cabins and store — grew from a log cabin wayside built in the 1880s on the military road that led from the Rogue River Valley to the Klamath Lake country.

Freight wagons hauling supplies to Fort Klamath made Union Creek a stopping place. Eventually a man named Woodruff built a log cabin and he and his family lived there, catering as best they could to travelers who came in buckboards and buggies loaded with camping supplies, headed for Diamond Lake, Crater Lake and Huckleberry Mountain. Woodruff built the first rough road to Huckleberry Mountain, the place that attracted both Indians and whites for the late summer huckleberry season.

In 1921 a man named Ed Beckelhymer built a garage and delicatessen at Union Creek and several years later James Grieves built a store. In 1927 Ed Regnier bought out Grieves, and the following year he built a lodge and cabins. The construction of Crater Lake Highway was making travel easier, and the trip into this difficult country was now possible for more people. Beckelhymer continued to operate the delicatessen, Becky's Cafe, and the garage.

In the spring of 1936 Regnier's lodge burned and construction was started on the lodge that now stands. One of the outstanding features of the new building was the stone fireplace in the lobby, built of opalized wood hauled to Union Creek from near Lakeview. It remains today as a point of interest in the long pine-paneled room.

The Union Creek Resort has catered to many changes in travel and traffic, but has managed to retain the special charm of a place of leisure in a hurried world.

NOTES

BUCK ROCK TUNNEL

Buck Rock Tunnel, ca. 1985.

BUCK ROCK TUNNEL

Buck Rock Tunnel has become an almost legendary railroad tunnel in the Siskiyou Mountains. Not many people have seen the dark and silent hole that pierces the solid rock ridge between Carter and Emigrant Creeks in the Buckhorn Springs country east of Ashland. This is because for many years the tunnel was considered "lost" and when it was "found," it was necessary to hike, stumble and push your way uphill through heavy underbrush to get there.

The railroad line connecting San Francisco to Portland was built from California north and from Portland south, the tracks meeting in Ashland in 1887. The event was important across the nation because it marked completion of the circle of railroads around the United States.

Buck Rock Tunnel was to have been Tunnel 13 on the line the Oregon and California Railroad Company was building between Hornbrook and Ashland, but it didn't turn out that way.

The Siskiyou Mountains posed a formidable natural barrier and construction engineer Samuel S. Montague (the town of Montague just out of Yreka, California, is named for him) thought it best to tunnel through at a low elevation to eliminate miles of winding track and steep grades. Work was started on Buck Rock Tunnel, south of Ashland, in November of 1883.

Several hundred Chinese were employed on the project — their construction camp at the site was called Hell Town — working with black powder before the perfection of dynamite.

Homesteaders cut and stacked wood nearby to be used for fuel for the steam engines they believed would soon chug and wheeze through the 1,650-foot tunnel that had progressed some 300 feet into the rocky ridge.

Word to stop construction came in February of 1884, and soon it was reported that John A. Hulburt, another O&C engineer, was surveying a grade to a Siskiyou Summit tunnel.

And then the Oregon and California company experienced financial difficulties, and was sold to the Central Pacific Railroad Company, which did some surveying but also had financial problems. The Southern Pacific Railroad Company came into possession of the holdings.

William Hood, a Southern Pacific engineer who had established his reputation for construction of the famous loop in the Techachapi Pass country of California, was put in charge of building the line over the Siskiyou Mountains. He announced that the company would "push along to the Siskiyou Mountain Tunnel Route" and that the Buck Rock Tunnel would be abandoned. The new tunnel would be Tunnel 13, Hood said, and it would pierce Siskiyou summit just above Coles Station. (You can see the approach to the tunnel just above Interstate 5, at the Mt. Ashland interchange.)

The first train passed through Tunnel 13 — destined to be the scene of the DeAutremont brothers train robbery in 1923 — on October 10, 1887, and the connecting spike on the Southern Pacific's San Francisco-Portland line was driven in Ashland two months later, on December 17. Buck Rock Tunnel, the big, black hole in the Buckhorn Springs country was forgotten. The fact that it was started was remembered only by a few.

"Buck Rock Tunnel was denied its birthright. It was never to feel the rumble and vibrations of the thundering steam engines or the tremor of the moaning diesels. The heavy freight and the people of a growing Oregon passed its portals, but never through. It was forgotten in the onward rush except by the few who seek it out and give it a place in history," wrote Mark Lawrence, a forester with the Bureau of Land Management in Medford, who in the 1950s set out to locate the tunnel entrance.

Lawrence had heard of the "lost" tunnel and tried several times without success to find it. After almost seventy years the forest hid the entrance well. Finally, by studying aerial photos of the terrain, Lawrence found what he believed were the grades leading to the opening, and in 1964 he and his sons found what they hunted for, a railroad-sized hole in the steep mountainside.

He wanted to know more about the history of the tunnel but could find no one to tell him the story. Only hearsay and legend repeated by oldtime railroaders over caboose coffee were to be found.

Lawrence went to the Jacksonville Museum and read the microfilm of all the local newspapers published between 1880 and 1887. He found snatches of information here and there, notes and paragraphs which he pieced together. He wrote the story of Buck Rock Tunnel which subsequently was published in "Our Public Land," a Bureau of Land Management publication, and in "Siskiyou Sites and Sagas," a booklet published by the Siskiyou Pioneer Sites Foundation.

Lawrence found that twenty-four years had elapsed between the time the preliminary surveys for a route over the mountain were made and the time the railroad line was finished. When the railroad lines joined in Ashland, some people still contended that the Buck Rock Tunnel route would have been the better of the two. Although two and one-half miles longer than the route chosen, it followed a two percent grade instead of a three percent grade, and it would have been on the sunny, frost-free side of the slopes.

Why the shorter but steeper and more expensive route was chosen is not known, but Lawrence says some believe the steeper route was a source of trouble that was largely responsible in later years for the Southern Pacific decision to construct another north-south line through Klamath Falls.

FINDING BUCK ROCK TUNNEL

Finding Buck Rock Tunnel remains a challenge. You should be prepared to drive, hike, and hunt, and you should carry with you a United States Geological Survey Siskiyou Pass Quadrangle topographic map.

Follow Oregon 66 east from Ashland nine miles to Buckhorn Springs Road. Turn right on Buckhorn Springs Road, at four-tenths of a mile turn right again on Emigrant Creek Road and follow it as it gradually climbs through the foothills. The road rounds a corner and affords you a view of Buck Rock on the forested skyline (make a mental note that Mark Lawrence says, "Buck Rock Tunnel is a half mile due south of Buck Rock as the crow flies over the poison oak") then continues up and along a ridge where it soon offers an excellent view of the open slopes of the Green Springs Mountain on your left.

At two and one-half miles from Oregon 66 an unmarked but easy to identify timber access road intersects on the right. Off-road parking space is on the left, and I suggest that you leave your car here and hike on in carrying your maps with you. It is approximately two miles to the tunnel entrance by way of the timber access road, a road that may not be regularly maintained and may be rough, washed out or for some other reason impassable.

As you walk along this road remember your general direction is straight ahead. You will pass a road that intersects from the left, and at approximately one mile in you will come to a Y in the road. Follow the right fork straight ahead. You have about one mile more to go. You will come to an intersection where the road branches right and rather steeply downhill. Stay on the left branch that hugs the contour of the mountainside.

The first indication that you are nearing the end of your trek is when, after walking through the forest with only occasional glimpses of Interstate 5 and the railroad on the Siskiyou Mountains, you come to an opening where your view of these landmarks is unobstructed.

Continue to follow the road until you see tailings — rock blasted and removed from the mountain during construction of the tunnel — covering the steep hillside to your left. At the extreme right edge of the tailings look up and you will see the trace of a narrow trail that cuts across and upward, from right to left. Follow this trail up to the old railroad grade — after one hundred years it more closely resembles a ditch — and turn left. The entrance to Buck Rock Tunnel is just ahead.

128

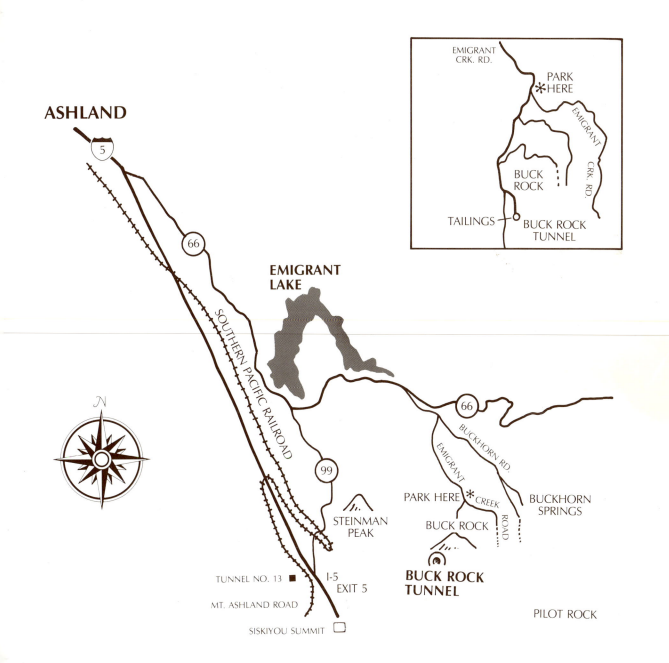

ASHLAND

EMIGRANT
LAKE

EMIGRANT
CRK. RD.

PARK
*HERE

EMIGRANT CRK. RD.

BUCK
ROCK

TAILINGS

BUCK ROCK
TUNNEL

SOUTHERN PACIFIC RAILROAD

N

66

66

99

BUCKHORN RD.

EMIGRANT CREEK ROAD

PARK HERE *

BUCKHORN
SPRINGS

STEINMAN
PEAK

BUCK ROCK

TUNNEL NO. 13 ■

I-5
EXIT 5

MT. ASHLAND ROAD

SISKIYOU SUMMIT

BUCK ROCK
TUNNEL

PILOT ROCK

COLESTIN

Colestin mineral water was promoted by the Southern Pacific Railroad Company, ca. 1890.

COLESTIN

Around the turn of the century excursion trains carried people who were enthusiastic about "healthful living" to Colestin and its mineral waters of "superior medicinal properties."

Leland Stanford, railroad builder and founder of Stanford University, said the water was so refreshing it was "slightly intoxicating." Trains chugged to a stop while passengers, tents, bags and baggage were unloaded on the small wooden railroad platform marked with the sign Colestin.

Families tented — as many as one hundred at a time — under the tall fir, pine and cedar trees, or stayed in the hotel that could accommodate twenty-five guests.

Everyone drank the mineral water, first thing in the morning, all day long, last thing at night. It was described as having "considerable iron content and heavily charged with carbonic acid." It was compared to Congress water at Saratoga Springs in New York.

Boys met the trains and filled demijohns with the water for the refreshment of passengers and crewmen. It was bottled and shipped to many parts of the country to be mixed with syrup for soft drinks.

The main gathering place for visitors at Colestin was the hotel. Framework for the two-story building built in 1881 was hewn from standing timber, the lengths pinned with round hardwood pins. Foundation underpinning was cut from the heart of red cedar and surface charred before it was used, and the 650 bannister rounds that formed the railings for the porch were turned out by hand with a lathe. Lumber for the floors and walls was cut in a nearby mill powered by an overshot waterwheel, and hand cut sugar pine shakes were used for the roof. A stone fireplace heated the dining room.

Mrs. Alice Rawlings, a granddaughter of Mr. and Mrs. Byron Cole who developed the resort on their property, lived in Medford in the 1960s. She remembered the sparkling prism-hung kerosene chandeliers that lighted the hotel and the special pieces of furniture her grandmother brought from the east — big wicker chairs, a cradle (nine of the Coles' ten children were born at Colestin), a trundle bed, and her grandmother's spinning wheel.

Colestin had fun and laughter aplenty. The dance band from the Italian colony at nearby Hilt, California, came for evening and weekend parties. The spot was a favorite of artists who set up their easels under the trees.

Colestin flourished as a resort until the mid-1920s. Recalling many happy days spent there as a child, Mrs. Rawlings said faster, easier highway travel spelled the end to railroad excursion trips to resorts such as Colestin.

Railroad excursion trips to Colestin were popular, ca. 1915.

Trappers and hunters knew of the mineral springs in the 1840s and were aware that deer and all hoofed animals came here to drink. Horses approaching the spot would break into a trot to reach the water, but clawed animals would not drink it. Even thirsty dogs avoided the springs.

Indians apparently did not drink the water although they came to Buckhorn Mineral Springs just a few miles over the Siskiyou Mountains. No sign of an Indian encampment has been found near Colestin even though the Indian trail passed over Siskiyou summit not far east of the springs. The trail skirted the entire springs area.

In 1851 Byron Cole and his brother Rufus left New York and came west to take up a donation land claim in the southeasternmost part of the Oregon Territory.

Byron returned east in 1860, married, and brought his bride to Oregon. The couple settled on 900 acres of land known as Upper Coles, and developed a prosperous cattle ranch. When the toll road was built over the Siskiyou Mountains in 1867, the Rufus Cole home on the original land claim became a stage stop called Cole's Station.

The Coles later purchased 320 acres of land that included the mineral springs. They decided to develop a resort based on the drawing power of the "healthful water" and the knowledge that the railroad would pass through the property. They started to build the hotel and in the same year a post office was established to serve the mill owners, saloon keepers, ranchers, teamsters and merchants who had located along the stage route.

In 1887 the Southern Pacific Railroad's north-south lines connected in Ashland. To encourage travel in the west the company undertook a program of promotion and advertised Colestin in its magazine, Sunset, and in other media, describing the mineral springs as having "superior medicinal properties."

People came from far and near. Colestin also was a popular place with the people of the Rogue River Valley.

Cole died in 1894 and Mrs. Cole continued to operate the resort until 1900 when she rented the property. Colestin was sold to Gust and George Avgeris, Greek immigrants, in 1925. They operated the ranch for many years, marketed cheese from their herd of goats and sold bottled mineral water.

Eventually the Avgeris family moved from the property. In the 1970s the area began to see an influx of newcomers who preferred free style rural living to the conventions of city subdivisions.

A SCENIC DRIVE

The resort is no more. Private homes now are scattered through the forest lying in the shadows of Mt. Ashland. A drive through the Colestin area is possible, however, and scenic. From the slopes of the Siskiyou Mountains you break out of the forest into foothills and meadows lying at the narrowing end of the long valley where the lumber mill community of Hilt once stood.

To make this drive, follow Interstate 5 south to the Mt. Ashland interchange, Exit 5. Turn right on the Mt. Ashland Ski Area road and follow it for approximately one mile to where the Colestin Road intersects on the left.

The Colestin Road is not paved but relatively well maintained. It follows the old Siskiyou Wagon Road route as it winds through the forest. Four miles from the ski area road Colestin Road crosses the railroad track. This is where the passenger platform marked Colestin once stood, and if you look back as you cross the tracks, you will catch a glimpse of the old hotel building.

Magnificent views of Mt. Shasta in the distance, and of open, rolling fields in the foreground are part of the pleasure of this trip as the road meanders through the oak studded lower reaches of the Siskiyous, into Cottonwood Creek Canyon, through the S.S. Bar Ranch, and past the Cole ranch house that served as a stage stop (1859-1887) on the Siskiyou Wagon Road.

Little remains to mark the townsite of Hilt — several homes, the community building, a church, a boarded-up school. Everything else was razed when Fruit Growers Supply Company closed the mill in 1973. The road continues through the Cottonwood Creek valley to connect with Interstate 5 at the Hilt interchange on the California side of the Siskiyou Mountains.

136

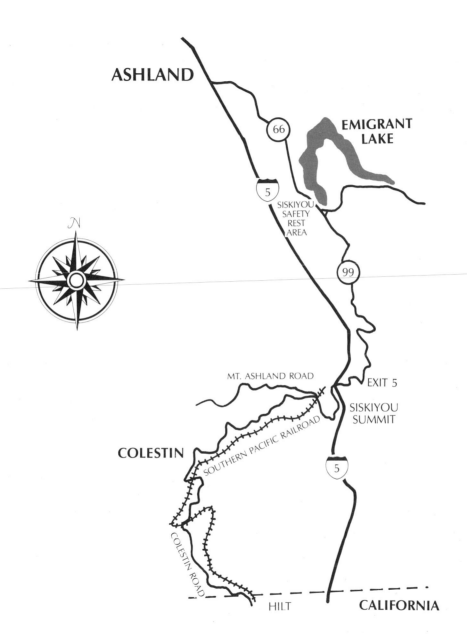

ASHLAND

EMIGRANT
LAKE

66

5

SISKIYOU
SAFETY
REST
AREA

99

N

MT. ASHLAND ROAD

EXIT 5

SISKIYOU
SUMMIT

COLESTIN

SOUTHERN PACIFIC RAILROAD

5

COLESTIN ROAD

HILT

CALIFORNIA

THE BLUE LEDGE MINE

At the Blue Ledge Mine, ca. 1910.

THE BLUE LEDGE MINE

Dynamite explosions rumbled along the misty blue skyline of the Siskiyou Mountains. The year was 1906. The word was copper. In a bustling mining camp known as Blue Ledge miners were drilling into what was believed to be the principal copper lode in a district encompassing more than 2,000 square miles.

Freight wagons pulled by teams of six and eight horses stirred up clouds of dust as they hauled machines and supplies from Medford through Jacksonville, the Applegate River country and up Joe Creek to the mining camp three miles into California. Two stages a day carried passengers and mail over the road that was the only outlet to what was said to be "beyond any question, the greatest body of copper in the west."

The quantity of ore blocked out in the Blue Ledge district in the early 1900s was described as "beyond calculation, only a prospect of what is in the future."

Talk in Medford was of building a railroad line to the area where more than a thousand claims had been located along ten parallel ledges that occupied a strip ten miles wide and twenty-five miles long.

Medford was booming in those years. It included three new bank buildings, eight new business blocks, 300 new homes, three newspapers, ". . . no caste or social barriers, power to all towns in the central valley, a death rate of less than six percent per thousand, 5,000 acres of new orchards, and thrice-weekly mail to the farmers," according to a promotional pamphlet published by the Medford Commercial Club. Mining was expected to boost the blossoming economy of Southern Oregon.

The Blue Ledge Mining Company let it be known that it would spare no expense or effort to fully develop the property that ultimately would have a smelter and reduction works capable of processing at least 500 tons of ore daily.

The copper vein carried good value of gold and a fair share of silver and the entire copper region was covered with pine and fir that provided the needed construc-

141

tion materials. Joe Creek, Elliot Creek and the Big and Little Applegate Rivers furnished an abundance of water for power and for mining.

Company officials said the Blue Ledge was expected to employ several thousand men. At the same time work was underway nearby in the Bloomfield, Copper King, Blue Canyon, Reddy and Rodgers, Callaghan's group, Tom Cat, St. Albans, Morris and Wakefield, Tin Cup, Eglo, Kyiak, Jeldness, Silent Sam and other mines.

The Hotel Eileen, a boarding house that boasted steam radiators and gas chandeliers, was built near the Blue Ledge camp, as were other buildings — a bunkhouse, cookhouse, headquarters offices, assay office, diamond drill testing shop, a dance hall, homes for the superintendents, engineers and workers. Tent houses sprang up on the four-terraced mountainside and a barn was built to shelter horses and mules.

Nearly $2 million was spent to develop the copper ledge that had been dormant and unexplored since the Blue Ledge Mining Company located it in 1898.

Ledgers from November, 1906, through 1916 showed the pattern of rise and decline of the Blue Ledge. The monthly payrolls grew to $17,775 in February, 1907, and remained relatively steady through 1908. Freight bills ran $3,000 to $4,000 per month. Groceries and supplies (including such items as $5.75 for liquor and $6.30 for washing) were duly noted.

The company bought more mining claims.

The Blue Ledge mine was developed by more than 15,000 feet of drifts and raises including a series of adits (nearly horizontal passages from the surface) that penetrated a cliff-like slope. A steeply inclined passageway connecting a working place with a lower one extended 210 feet below the lowest adit, from which levels were turned at 100-foot intervals. These workings explored the deposit for a vertical distance of about 800 feet and an horizontal distance of about 2,000 feet.

Copper ore from the Blue Ledge was crushed, sacked and shipped to smelters in Tacoma, Washington. The mine was in the Squaw Creek mining district, which was credited with producing about $181,000 in copper ore. Estimates made by the U.S. Department of Interior geological survey later determined that approxi-

Blue Ledge mining camp, ca. 1920.

mately $2 million in copper was produced from mines in Southwest Oregon and Northern California just after the turn of the century, but the mines were not quite rich enough to pay for development. The deposits were big, but not big enough. The country was too broken up. In Arizona entire tops of mountains were being removed and ore was being mined with power shovels. This was cheaper and faster, and more ore could be recovered.

The year 1908 brought trouble to the nation and to the Blue Ledge Mine. Banks across the United States closed. The government did what it could to help develop the west, but the next few years were not years of general prosperity.

Dr. J. F. Reddy, a geologist, promoter and mining engineer, was sent to Southern Oregon to consider further development of the Blue Ledge. Two types of ore were found, a low grade pyritic and a better grade copper-zinc. More holes were drilled and more crosscuts made, but the main body of the pyritic ore never was opened. Freight rates were high, labor costs were high, the price paid for copper remained the same. A brief surge of renewed interest occurred, but not enough to warrant a full-scale operation. By 1919 the mine closed, buildings, machines and equipment were dismantled.

A great deal of ore was, however, left blocked out in the Blue Ledge or stored in dumps. Assay maps indicated more than 150,000 tons of ore were still available in the mine.

"The Blue Ledge contains ore which will be valuable when metal prices rise again high enough to offset the costs of mining and smelting and the rather high cost of transportation," was the opinion expressed in the U.S. Department of Interior geological survey published in 1933.

Locally those who have been interested in mining development over the years have a variety of ideas: "The Blue Ledge has been kicked around by several big companies. . . . It has been held off the market on purpose as a sort of reserve deposit. . . . If the mine ever is opened again, it will be for zinc. . . . Sure, minerals will be important here again in the future."

But whether the skyline of the Siskiyou Mountains will ever see renewed interest in copper mining remains a question.

144

APPLEGATE LAKE

The Blue Ledge and its story are part of our past. The word in the Applegate River Valley today is recreation. For pastoral beauty, and for variety in things to see and do, the country held by the misty blue skyline of the Siskiyou Mountains is the place to go.

Follow Oregon 238 through Jacksonville to Ruch. Turn left on Upper Applegate Road. It is fourteen miles to Applegate Lake, but there are places to explore enroute.

Valley View Vineyard is just out of Ruch, and its tasting room is open daily. Cantrall Buckley Park is nearby, McKee Bridge — the historic covered bridge, picnic park and swimming area — a few miles up the road. Here also you will find Flumet Flat Campground and interpretive trail, and the Jackson Picnic Area. Watch for the roadside signs. Once you reach the lake, the recreational opportunities are many and varied. Along with day use and overnight campgrounds, you will find boat launching ramps and hiking trails with well marked trailheads. Brochures are available at the visitors center at the lake, at U.S. Forest Service offices in Medford and Ashland, and at Star Ranger Station on Upper Applegate Road.

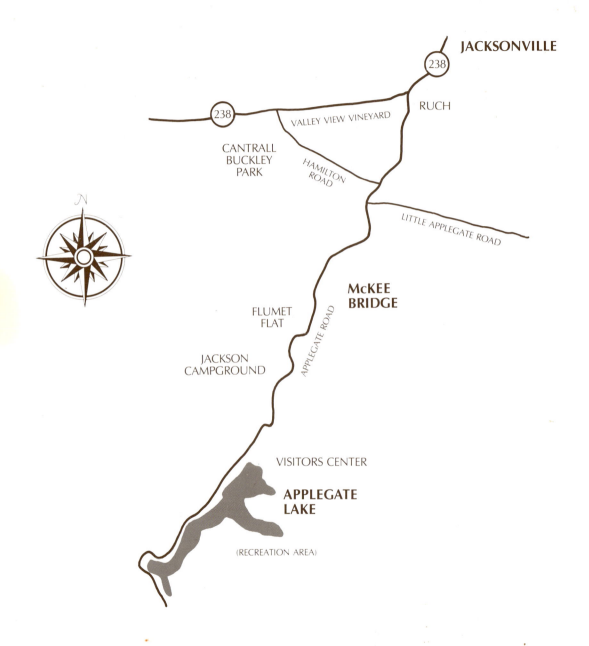

JACKSONVILLE

238

RUCH

VALLEY VIEW VINEYARD

CANTRALL
BUCKLEY
PARK

238

HAMILTON ROAD

LITTLE APPLEGATE ROAD

McKEE
BRIDGE

FLUMET
FLAT

APPLEGATE ROAD

JACKSON
CAMPGROUND

VISITORS CENTER

APPLEGATE
LAKE

(RECREATION AREA)

NOTES

THE TOKETEE COUNTRY

Toketee Falls.

THE TOKETEE COUNTRY

In Chinook jargon Toketee means pretty or graceful, and Lemolo means wild and untamed. And the Toketee country — a two and one-half hour drive from Medford — is just that.

This is the country of the North Umpqua River, a country of swift flowing streams, rocky gorges and quiet pools; a country of tall, green trees and quiet paths; a country of sparkling lakes — and not too many people.

Lemolo Lake, near the headwaters of the Umpqua, is about ten miles north of Diamond Lake, and Toketee Falls is another ten miles down the road. The highway, Oregon 138, is wide and smooth and generously dotted with scenic turnout points.

There are numerous forest camps, picnic areas and waysides, and place names that make you wonder — Rhododendron Ridge, Pig Iron Mountain, Dread and Terror Trail, Whitehorse Falls Camp, Maidu Lake Trail, Calamut Lake.

Dog Creek Indian Cave and the Kalmiopsis Area are within exploring distance of Toketee. The cave was discovered by white men in 1914 when Burley Wright, a homesteader, happened across it. It is one large room with three smaller depressions and has pictographs on the walls. To get to the cave, hike in about three miles from the Dry Creek Store. It is a climb, not an easy walk. The trail passes the grave of Bill Bradley, the first white resident of the area, and opens up vista views of Mt. Bailey and Mt. Thielsen.

Kalmiopsis leachiana, a delicate lavender flower that botanists say is a survivor of the ice age, is found here between February and June. In the fall, the vine maples turn crimson.

Little was known about the Toketee country when John Boyle, an imaginative engineer for the California Oregon Power Company (later to merge with Pacific Power and Light Company) explored it on horseback in the early 1920s. Boyle believed that because of the drop of the North Umpqua River, electric power could

151

be produced with a series of plants on small holding lakes. This would not destroy the spectacular river channel as would one big plant on a large lake that would back up water for miles.

He advanced his idea through the proper channels and the result was one of the outstanding hydroelectric developments in the west, if not in the world. Engineers came from afar to study it.

The $57 million North Umpqua Project was started in 1947 and completed in 1956. Along with using the natural resources to provide power, it also opened up these places to the public.

The project resulted in the creation of Lemolo Lake, a reservoir that impounds the outflow of Diamond Lake, and in Clearwater Lake, where the Clearwater River rushes into the Umpqua River at Toketee Falls. Both lakes are popular with fishermen, swimmers and families wanting to camp where they can hike along forest trails.

For the camera enthusiast, spectacular rock formations offer plenty of challenge.

Eight hydro plants use the flow of the river and its tributary streams over and over again. Canals hug canyon walls and tunnels pierce mountain peaks. Huge penstocks plunge down sheer cliffs carrying water to generators — and a few hundred feet away, the forest looks almost primeval.

The production of power along this forty-two mile stretch of the river is in itself exciting enough to call for a visit.

If you camp, an overnight trip or longer is suggested. If you are interested in a one-day trip only, a loop drive from Medford to Diamond Lake then down the North Umpqua River Highway to Roseburg and home via Interstate 5 is recommended.

But don't hurry.

The Indians who told one another of the wild and beautiful country said it very well in Toketee and Lemolo.

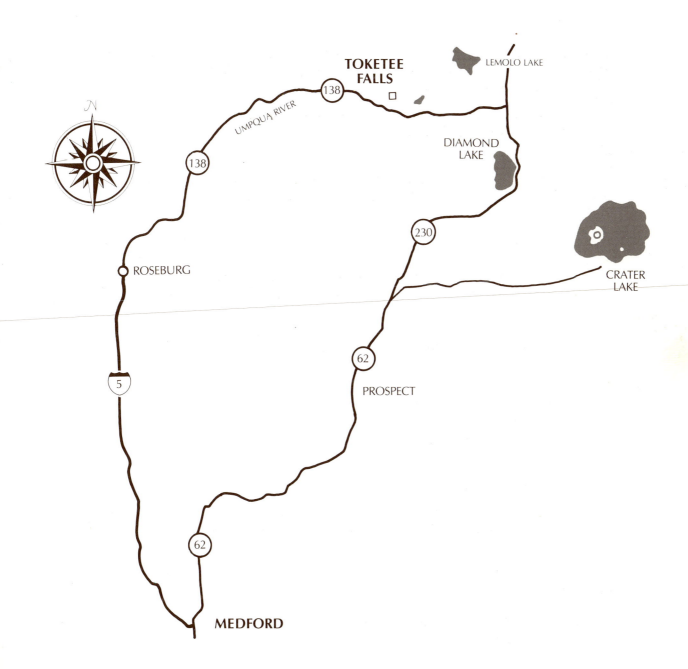

TOKETEE
FALLS

LEMOLO LAKE

UMPQUA RIVER

138

138

DIAMOND
LAKE

CRATER
LAKE

230

ROSEBURG

62

5

PROSPECT

62

MEDFORD

SHALE CITY

Defend Title

BIG RETORT IS PLACED IN OPERATION

Hartman Syndicate Produces First Oil From Ashland Shale Beds

RETORT RUN BY GAS

Minor Details to be Worked Out Before Plant is Started on Full-Time Production

Ashland has struck oil. Such was the announcement this morning of R. P. Campbell, who told a Tidings representative that after more than a year of work, the first crude oil had this morning been obtained from rock, through a Hartman ... the

Ashland Tidings carries the news.

SHALE CITY

On July 4, 1922, a crowd in Ashland pushed closer around a man who was demonstrating a machine he said could distill oil from rock.

H. W. Hartman set up his scale model "retort" on the Plaza. The machine churned, the sticky black stuff dripped, and no one turned away. Hartman explained that by a process that included crushing and heating oil-bearing shale, the retort could extract the valuable liquid. He told the crowd shale beds could be found not far from Ashland. His listeners were skeptical but open to being convinced.

Interest grew in the oil development idea when it became known in December that Hartman had invested $1,000 in shale land east of Ashland. More interest was seen when he purchased part of an adjacent section of land in February of the following year.

Soon thereafter Hartman formed a syndicate, and on May 28, 1923, he filed articles of incorporation. People were eager to buy into the oil venture. Capital stock was set at $3 million and the selling price was $10 per share. Cattlemen, farmers, lumbermen, bankers, merchants, and teachers — all thrilled to be in on the beginning of an era of great new wealth — invested their money in the Hartman Syndicate, Inc.

They joined forces and cut a road through the foothills country to the shale beds. They built a base of operations, a sawmill, school, store, cookhouse, shops, and houses, a community they called Shale City.

On April 22, 1924, Hartman and his wife moved to Shale City where he personally took charge of construction of the retort. It took several months to build the 250-ton machine that was to churn out the wealth.

Then Hartman announced in the Ashland Daily Tidings that the "first bit of gasoline to be manufactured in Oregon, as a purely Oregon product, has been manufactured from Ashland crude. The work was done in Portland by a chemical engineer of The Hartman Syndicate, Inc. The gasoline contains sufficient low boiling point fractions to meet the specifications officially adopted by the federal government."

The plant was being completed. Cement foundations for the retort were poured and a tower was built to receive the gear box drive. Railroad track was laid from the shale beds to the retort house and two bins with a capacity of 900 tons of shale each were completed.

The plan was to pass shale rock from railroad cars into bins, through a crusher and into the retort. From the retort, crude oil was to be piped into storage at the bottom of the hill.

Steam shovels began to open up the shale beds. It was time for a general meeting of the stockholders.

"It is exceedingly gratifying to note that you, as stockholders, stand solidly behind the institution," Hartman told the group. He explained that trust and support were indicated by the fact that every measure calling for a vote had been passed unanimously.

Hartman was elected treasurer and general manager of the corporation. As treasurer he announced, "No financial statement will be given at this time owing to the fact the books are still with the public accountant."

On May 26, 1924, E. W. Hartman, inventor of the retort and brother of the syndicate head, arrived in Ashland. He was present when the big machine was started up and all the businessmen connected with the syndicate were invited to Shale City to see the retort in operation.

Headlines of July 29, 1924, announced, "Ashland Has Struck Oil — The first crude oil was this morning obtained from shale rock through a Hartman Retort."

The highest expectations were exceeded when the retort, built to handle a daily capacity of 250 tons of rock, used 600 tons and produced 1,260 gallons of crude oil.

Then the retort idled. Additional machinery was necessary the Hartman brothers explained.

Late in August a bigger condenser was ordered and in September the machinery again was started briefly before being "shut down for adjustment."

Late in September the curiosity of everyone in the area was aroused when three Japanese visitors arrived in Ashland. No one seemed to know why they were in town. They departed and several days later a news report, secured via a London source, was repeated by Hartman. The report indicated, he said, that Japan was interested in developing oil shale deposits in Manchuria to get oil for the Japanese navy. The report mentioned the shale operation in Ashland.

Stockholders hardly could wait to get the big machine in continuous operation. Their time and efforts soon were to be rewarded and their investment secured.

And then, less than two weeks later, the beautiful dream of riches was shaken.

On September 27, 1924, an attack was made on the Hartman Syndicate by Governor Pierce's stock investigating committee. An investigation apparently had been ordered to prevent the issuance of one and one-half million shares of stock to Hartman. The investigation was expected to show that the Hartman Syndicate had issued three million shares of stock with half the amount to be held in escrow by H. W. Hartman for promotion work.

The investigating committee charged that the syndicate "apparently organized for the purpose of creating a market for certain equipment used in the extraction of oil from rock, with said equipment manufactured by other concerns in which Hartman was heavily interested."

The report charged that the promoters were to receive $1,500,000 of the $3,000,000 capital stock with the public "expected to supply the capital and assume the risks."

Two days later Hartman's attorney replied and on October 9, 1924, Hartman filed a suit against Oswald West and George Black, members of the governor's stock investigating committee. The suit sought $100,000 for alleged libel.

On October 14, trying to hold on to their dreams, stockholders "voiced confidence still," in the venture, and on November 6, they held a special meeting during which they examined the books and financial reports.

"The company, recently, because of inability to sell stock in this state following an attack made on the company several months ago, has been handicapped by a lack of finances which has directed criticism and semi-legal actions against the company," was the statement published in the newspaper following the November meeting.

Hartman left on what he said would be a brief business trip to New York. On November 11, hopes of the stockholders were strengthened when Hartman telegraphed that ample cash for work would be assured with the sale of stock in New York. He would remain in the East and handle all transactions.

Four days later supplemental articles of incorporation were filed.

On February 9, 1925, the syndicate was granted a twenty-year oil shale lease from the U.S. Department of Interior for 2,680 acres of public domain land, in accordance with the Congressional Act of 1920 to promote mining of coal, phosphates, oil, oil shale, gas, and sodium, on public domain lands.

On March 4 a telegram was received from Hartman who was still in New York. It read, "Have arranged finances to take care of all our obligations; one half to be paid in thirty days, the balance in sixty days. Am sending a man to Ashland the first of the month to put the plant in operation."

The telegram brought renewed encouragement to those interested in the venture. It was, however, the last word to be received directly from Hartman. No further personal mention of Hartman or of his direct actions is found in the records. Where he went, what he did, no one seems to know.

Stockholders decided to run the lumber mill at Shale City to work out liquidation of as many local accounts as possible. Firewood was cut and delivered in partial payment of many debts.

On August 15, 1925, notice was filed in circuit court to dismiss or proceed with the $100,000 libel suit the Hartman Syndicate had brought against the governor's committee. Outside of filing the original complaint, no legal action had been taken and the court, to clear the docket, issued the notice.

Seven months later there was an unexpected turn of events when a Los Angeles man, who identified himself as the president of a "reorganized Hartman syndicate," announced, "The 250-ton retort is to be put into operation within sixty or ninety days. For the last several months a series of experiments has been made with a retort in Los Angeles. The results assure success . . ."

Under the reorganization plan, he said, the new capital that was interested in the shale oil industry would go ahead only on condition that creditors declare a temporary moratorium. What money was available for the industry was to be used exclusively for development work for the time being. Later, he explained, the company "confidently expects" to be on a firm financial basis and able to take care of debts.

Stockholders believed they had too much invested to quit.

On June 24, 1926, supplemental articles of incorporation were filed changing the name to Pacific Lumber and Shaleries, Inc. Two years of work followed. The retort was rebuilt and employes were paid in stock. Once again the endeavor seemed headed down the path to fortune.

The work was completed, shale bins were full, the big machine was started, and then — before horrified eyes — it melted into a pile of junk.

And that was it.

Gone were six years of hard work, gone were the savings of those who had seen such a bright future in oil, gone were the hopes of wealth for families and community, and gone was the man with the oil machine.

In 1930 the president of Pacific Lumber and Shaleries, Inc. decided to make one last effort. He was enroute to Salem in an attempt to secure backing for another try when he was killed in an automobile accident.

Some Ashland residents wonder still, "Should we have given it just one more chance?"

A portion of the shale beds was worked in the 1960s by a California company that shipped several railroad carloads of the rock south each year and processed it into a soil conditioning compound.

The Shale City Road trip is described on Pages 78-80. Stay on the road and enjoy the scenery. Shale City is no more, the buildings are gone, the property is privately owned.

Shale City Road.

NOTES

Little Nick.

LITTLE NICK

"We called him Nick," rancher Jim Bell said. "I often wondered if we had been right in taking freedom away from such an animal. God had given him a stout heart, a fearless disposition and the courage to make decisions. Who were we to change the life he loved so well?"

In the spring of 1930 Bell was riding for cattle near Buck Rock in the foothills of the Siskiyou Mountains.

"Everything was very much alive," he said as he drifted back to the first day he saw Nick. "The sunshine was warm, the new grass was turning the country-side green, wildflowers bloomed everywhere and the oak trees were getting new leaves. I rode into an opening and saw one of the wild mares we knew had been running with the herd. She had a colt at her side, a little black rascal only a couple of days old but very much alive. He had all the joy of a thing born free. He didn't look as though he would ever grow into a horse big enough for a man to ride.

"I left him, but I didn't forget him."

From time to time the black colt would be seen, a streak out of the brush across an open glade.

"He never seemed to touch the ground, he just floated with his head and tail held high. He had developed a good set of legs, a short back and a beautiful, proud head," Bell said, "but he was a wild one."

Neighboring ranchers wanted him shot.

"I don't want that knot-headed stallion running with my bunch," a cattleman told Bell. "I've told my riders to shoot him if they see him."

But they never got close enough to carry out the orders.

Two years passed and the wily little black horse grew. He had the cunning of a fox and the cleverness of a deer. When he was chased, he headed for the bedrock where he left no tracks, disappearing in manzanita thickets.

"He would jump fences too high for saddle horses. By chasing him they were only teaching him to leave the band and find hiding places," Bell said.

"My admiration for that little rascal grew. I wanted him. 'He'll kill you, Jim,' the others said. 'He's wild, not worth the bother,' but I had to get to know that horse better."

The day finally came. The ranchers got the band of horses between two fences where there were no bedrock ridges or manzanita thickets and when the dust cleared, the little black was in the corral.

"When he realized what had happened, he lunged for the gate," Bell said. "I slammed it in his face. He whirled like a devil in a fury, and circled first one way and then the other with his head cocked to the side. I called out, 'Settle down, little Nick.' Then I had the thrill of my life. I opened the gate and stepped inside the corral. I expected to see Nick dash and throw himself against the side or come at me open-mouthed, but he didn't. He didn't flick an eyelid. He looked me square in the eye and there was no fear. He shook that proud head gently up and down as much as to say, 'All right, I'm trapped, but let's have this understood. You treat me right and I'll treat you right.' "

Training the stallion was not easy, but it wasn't too long before all Bell had to do was speak sharply to him when he did something wrong, caress him with voice or stroke when he did something right.

"It was a case of encouraging the good habits and discouraging the bad," Bell said. "In a short time he was responding well.

"I worked with him for an hour every day in the log corral we built for him. He needed exercise so my wife Ada took over the job of leading him into the fields every day. She let him eat where the grass was best and pulled handsful of green alfalfa and oats for him.

"Nick grew to worship Ada. He followed her like a dog. He was her jealous protector. He would come running when she called to him and put his head on her shoulder.

"I broke him to the saddle and gave him to her."

Nick was still a small horse and the other ranchers shook their heads and wondered why Bell chose him to ride on a cattle gathering. When Bell saddled Nick, they accused him of riding a saddle and a blanket with four legs under it.

"I see a head sticking out on one end. I wonder if there is a tail on the other," they joshed. "Get off and pack him, Jim, you are bigger than he is," they chided.

"But they didn't laugh for long," Bell said. "Nick and I jumped two wild yearlings, and they headed for the tall and uncut. Nick seemed to sense what was wanted and he tore after them, staying with them and beating them at every turn. Those critters were moving and we were right after them. We got within hollering distance of the corral and I yelled for an open gate. We popped out of the brush in sight of the riders fanned out on either side of the gate.

"We didn't need any help. The little horse they had made fun of was putting on a real show. Those yearlings couldn't out-dodge him. Nick set his feet and slid through the gate with their tails flapping right under his chin.

"I felt good inside. I felt good all over, and I couldn't help a big grin. I looked around at that circle of faces. No one said a word. Awe and admiration were written there.

"I headed for the barn to change horses. Nick had done enough. He moved like he was walking on air with his head held high. He had shown those cattlemen he wasn't something to take lightly; he was a horse to reckon with.

"As we crossed the creek, I heard one rancher say, 'I don't know what that is Jim is riding, but whatever it is, it's got fire in it.' "

In time, with good care and feed, Nick filled out to be a 950-pound beauty. And then on one of those warm, spring-like days, some memory stirred within him and he jumped the fence and headed back to the open range.

"Ada and I wondered what we should do," Bell said. "I remembered the look Nick had given me that day in the corral, the day he lost his freedom. Did we have the right to take that away from him again?

"I took a halter from the barn and started out after him. I found him in a little glade, standing with his old range pals.

" 'The decision is yours, Nick,' I said as I held out the halter. He looked at me. I waited. I whistled softly to remind him. I waited. He took a few steps toward me then he backed off. He turned his head to look at the other horses. He looked back at me.

"Four times he did this. I waited. I whistled softly. Then Nick came and put his nose in the halter. I buckled it and we hit the trail for home. He never tried to leave us again."

Jim and Ada Bell lived on a ranch off Buckhorn Springs Road. There is no short trip suggestion to go along with the story of the little wild horse they tamed and loved. It is included in this collection because it is one of my favorites. MO'H

Jim and Ada Bell.

Charlie Hoover.

CHARLIE HOOVER, THE TREE MAN

In 1959 Charles C. Hoover placed a tiny tree in the hands of a child and said, "This tree is your very own, forever. Plant it and care for it and someday, when you get to be an old cowpoke like me, you'll come back to this beautiful valley and look up at a big tree and you'll remember the day you planted it, and you will know that it is still your very own."

This story is included in this collection because Mr. Hoover was right. Many beautiful trees decorate the Rogue Valley today that children, now grown, remember planting.

Charlie Hoover and his wife Elsie, who lived on a ranch near Central Point, distributed more than a million trees in Oregon, Washington, California, Arizona, New Jersey, Kansas and New Mexico. They worked with youngsters in school and church groups, with Boy Scout and Girl Scout troops and with garden clubs.

Their dream was "to make this whole country look like a lovely park," and they did what they could to make their dream come true.

After the first trees were distributed and planted in Jackson County, the program reached into the three neighboring counties.

Hoover enjoyed it. He said he "warmed up to an idea that struck my fancy," and decided to go into the work on an all-out basis, letting the children, "our most important crop," help.

He started to place orders for trees — thousands at a time.

When the trees were delivered to his home, he and Mrs. Hoover worked with a group of youngsters who came to prepare the seedlings for distribution. Each was packaged in a compost mixture. The work was done on an assembly line basis. The trees were then taken to schools where they were distributed and many were given to garden clubs for planting.

Hoover made a little ceremony out of the school presentations, telling the children how to plant and care for the trees, and how to arrange the various kinds so the colors would blend.

In return for his gifts he received thousands of thank you letters, which he considered his most prized possessions. "As the program grew, I started to receive letters in big bundles," he said. "I read and kept every one of them." Because his work received nationwide attention, local postmasters learned where to send letters simply addressed to "Mr. Hoover, Southern Oregon."

Requests came in. People in states other than Oregon wanted trees, and they got them, just for the asking.

Mr. and Mrs. Hoover distributed more than sixty-five varieties of trees including all types of spruce, incense cedar, locust, white birch, northern red oak, pin oak, Chinese elm, Russian olive, weeping willow, redwood, dogwood and the beautiful green ash, the state tree of North Dakota.

They traveled to her home country, Greenwood County, Kansas, where they distributed 16,000 trees in token of memories and friendship.

Hoover, who was born in Grants Pass in 1890, maintained that "all a good man needs to get on his feet is a water hole, a patch of grass, and a wood pile."

Early in his career he was a nursery salesman. Then he operated a dairy farm. His ranching career started with Ed Hanley on the Hanley Ranch, and one thing led to another.

Hoover explained by saying, "Sometimes I would get ideas, then I would just have to try things."

He began experimenting with grasses and in the 1920s he developed a hardy winter bluegrass, a grass that added five months to late fall and early spring pastures. The grass was shipped to all parts of the world and still is widely used.

Hoover was one of the original growers of Ladino clover for seed and he was also the first grower to use an airplane for grass seeding and crop and animal dusting. He built experimental lakes on the soil of Southern Oregon's Agate Desert (White City area) and turned dry acres into productive land that he later subdivided.

His studies and discoveries were closely watched and drew worldwide attention from agricultural experts. In the 1950s he was honored by the Oregon Seed Industry, which named him one of the Top Ten Seed Pioneers in Oregon.

And then came the day for retirement, the day Hoover decided to let his two sons take over the farm properties.

"When you close down that old desk, you're done," the rancher said. "There is just no more use for a man who runs out of things to do. Me? I started this tree-planting program."

When asked about the expense involved in giving away more than a million trees, Hoover shook his head and said:

"That isn't important. We won't talk about it. The important thing is to make trees available to those who want them. This is what Elsie and I wanted to do."

Charles and Elsie Hoover.

MT. ASHLAND

On the summit of Mt. Ashland, ca. 1930.

MT. ASHLAND

One of the nice things about going to Mt. Ashland in the summertime is that nobody expects you to ski. You can drive up, enjoy the scenery, have a picnic, and that's as far as things athletic are concerned.

It takes less than an hour to drive to the Mt. Ashland Ski Area from Medford via Interstate 5 and the Mt. Ashland Road (Interstate 5, Exit 5). It is a trip recommended for days when the valleys are heat-wilted and August brown, and you are ready for cooler air.

The road is paved to the ski area. From Interstate 5 it cuts along the California side of the Siskiyou Mountains and you can look down on the valleys that shelter Colestin Springs, Hilt and Hornbrook. Mt. Shasta, always magnificent, dominates the skyline.

The higher the road climbs, the greener the low shrubs and grass, the more stately the forest trees. The air is fresh and full of the fragrance of wildflowers. The sky is especially blue. The parking lot at the ski lodge looks strangely empty compared with wintertime when it is filled to overflowing with cars and skiers, and the ski slopes look even steeper than when they are covered with snow.

The road from the lodge to the peak of the mountain is not paved and may be dusty, but the experience is worth it. Where access roads intersect, stay right on the main road.

Wildflowers grow in profusion along the sides of the road and a Forest Service picnic area — with tables, fireplaces and restrooms — is located about a mile from the lodge. It has been designed around a castle-like formation of granite boulders. Chipmunks chatter as they scamper from rock to rock and you sometimes see deer grazing nearby.

Past the picnic area the road cuts across a sloping alpine meadow at an elevation of about 7,000 feet. The main road continues on, but an intersecting road veers to the right to start the steep winding climb to the peak. Follow it. The ground

181

cover is rocks — small and large, some glistening white granite and others covered with rich black lichen — interspersed with diminutive but hardy multi-colored blooming things.

This is a part of the Siskiyou Mountains area that has been known as a botanist's paradise since the early 1800s when David Douglas, a Scot explorer, braved the west coast wilderness to collect seeds and plants. It is a geologically ancient area where more rare Alpine flowers and more varieties of lowland rock plant life are found than anywhere else in the world, although scientists never have determined exactly why.

And then you reach the windy ridge at the top of Mt. Ashland. Three structures — a television transmitter, weather radar station, and the ski hut at the top of the chair lift — are located there, but perhaps because of the wind, you still feel alone. It is not an unpleasant feeling; instead, it helps you understand why, since time began, people have been drawn to mountaintops.

As you stand here and enjoy the spectacular view, you are looking over the country of Buckhorn Springs, Bear Creek, Maryum's Rose, the place where little Nick ran free, the valley where children planted thousands of very special trees — you are looking over the country of SOUTHERN OREGON.

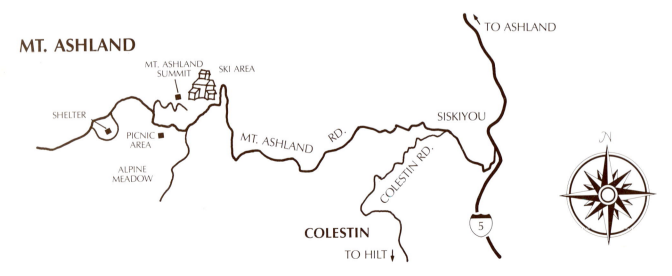

MT. ASHLAND

TO ASHLAND

MT. ASHLAND SUMMIT

SKI AREA

SHELTER

SISKIYOU

PICNIC AREA

MT. ASHLAND RD.

COLESTIN RD.

ALPINE MEADOW

5

COLESTIN

TO HILT

NOTES

MT. SHASTA

Mt. Shasta.

MT. SHASTA

Geographically, Mt. Shasta is outside the boundaries of this collection, and historically some of the spooky stories about California's mystery mountain strain credibility. But whether you drive to Mt. Shasta — it takes less than two hours from Medford, via Interstate 5 and the town of Mount Shasta — or simply enjoy it from a distance, the mountain has a story to tell.

Mt. Shasta is one of the most magnificent peaks on the Pacific slope.

Since the beginning of time it has been known for its strange atmosphere. Its history records stories of strange persons appearing and disappearing, of ghostly, glittering lights, of the sound of bells, of mighty chimes.

Mt. Shasta, rising 14,161 feet into the sky, is sixteen million years old. "Lonely as God and white as the winter moon," were the words the poet Joaquin Miller used to describe the mystic mountain.

Indian tribes living in the forested shadows of Mt. Shasta would not climb above the timberline because of their profound veneration for the "Great Spirit who dwells in this mountain with his people, as in a tent."

They believed the Great Spirit made the mountain by dropping ice and snow through an opening in the sky, then, wishing to remain on earth to make sea and more land, he converted the mountain into a wigwam and built a fire in the center.

Indian legend also told of the Shupchers, fierce giant-like people who lived in the region. Smoke belching from the summit of Mt. Shasta was believed to have come from a subterranean passage where Indian braves had built fires to flush out the giants.

And some of the dark-skinned people recognized the occult aspects of the mountain, believing it inhabited by a race of invisible people. They heard the musical laughter of children carried on the winds that swept the luminous ridges.

J. O. McKinney, a retired state agricultural inspector who lived in the community of Mount Shasta for more than twenty years, heard many of the legends of the mountain.

Shaking his head, he said, "There are a lot of weird stories about that mountain; most everyone who lives here has some sort of tale to tell. Believe them? Humph, not me." Then , growing more serious, he added, "But after all, who am I to say they are the bunk? There are some mighty intelligent, well-educated people who insist there is something very special about that mountain."

In the 1880s Frederick Spencer Oliver, a young man in his teens, claimed that while visiting the mountain he was chosen amanuensis (secretary) by Phylos The Thibetan, and instructed to take dictation for the book "A Dweller On Two Planets: or, The Dividing Of The Way," a book that became one of the first authorized occult classics.

Oliver claimed the interior of Mt. Shasta was "a mystic temple afar from the maddening crowd, a refuge whereof those who seeing, not see," the home of the Mystic Brotherhood Sach.

He described corridors excavated by giants, walls polished as jewels, and floors carpeted with fleecy gray fabric that looked like fur but was a mineral product. The key to the temple was, "One who first conquers self, Shasta will not deny," Oliver wrote.

Perhaps the best known legend of the mountain — and many people insist that rumors, myths and legends have their origin in a deep, underlying truth usually unrecognized by all but the real students of life — is the Lemurian legend.

Rudolph Steiner, a doctor of philosophy from Vienna, in his writings "Akashic Records" encouraged those who shared the belief that within Mt. Shasta live the remnants of the Lemurian race.

He said the Lemurians had lived in natural shelters, caves modified according to their needs, because of the presence of volcanoes on the continent of Lemuria.

The story as told in "Lemuria, The Lost Continent of the Pacific," published by the Rosicrucian Press in San Jose, California, in 1931, persists. Its origin was said to have been in manuscripts secured from ancient archives in Tibet and China.

Lemuria was once a great continent several thousand miles long and almost 2,000 miles wide in an area now covered by the Pacific Ocean. Its people, the world's oldest civilization, possessed supernatural power and knowledge.

When the continent, whose east shore was once part of the Cascade Range separated from North America by an inland sea, began to sink because of geologic changes in the surface of the earth, some of its people fled to the safety of a high peak, Mt. Shasta.

The Lemurians were described in the legend as being seven feet tall with large heads, high foreheads and long arms. Their most unusual feature was a protrusion in the center of their foreheads about the size and shape of a walnut, and this supposedly gave them a faculty of telepathy and communication with animals.

"I won't say it was a Lemurian," Archie McKillop, Medford guide, lumberman and skier once said, "but something followed me up on that mountain one night. I was with a party of skiers headed up to Horse Camp. I had gone on ahead to open the lodge and start the coffee. Suddenly I knew I was being followed. I could hear the crunch of the snow behind me, but I could see nothing.

"Whatever it was it stopped following me as I climbed above timberline. I had been at the cabin about half an hour when the second skier arrived white as a ghost. He told me he had been followed to the cabin door. We checked the area the next morning. There was no sign of anything human there."

Forest rangers and power company crewman who work in the forested lower reaches of the mountain also tell tales of Shasta — most of them concerning "strange little, old disappearing people wandering here for no apparent reason."

One of their favorite stories is of a bearded old man who lived in the mountain house at a place called Snowman's Hill. He claimed he put cornflakes out "for them." He claimed to have talked "with them." The busy crewmen enjoyed his stories but never pressed for details.

Stories of strange looking persons emerging from the forests then running back to hide — coming into a small community to trade gold for a commodity — reached far from the base of the mysterious mountain many years ago.

In 1932 the Los Angeles Times sent an investigator who related the stories he heard and described the phenomena he had witnessed.

He published the story and in summary wrote: "It is not, therefore, incredible that the last sons of the lost Lemuria are nestled at the foot of Mt. Shasta's volcano. The real incredible thing is that these staunch descendants of that vanished race have succeeded in secluding themselves in the midst of our teeming state."

Yet another legend, rumor or myth exists — another belief about the mystic mountain.

According to the initiated, the greatest bells in the world are the bells of the Secret Commonwealth of Mount Shasta and the great cities of Iletheleme and Yaktayvia, cities that lie beneath the vast mass of Mt. Shasta.

Yaktayvians are reputed to be the greatest bellmakers in the world. They employed the sound of bells and chimes to hollow out space for a city within the mountain. Corridors, galleries and tunnels are illuminated as continuous sound and vibrating atoms produce light.

On the northwest slope of Mt. Shasta is said to be a great transparent bell. It reflects no light and is invisible at a distance of more than eighteen inches. When the wind strikes it produces a sound so high pitched, it repels the curious and protects the entrance to the Secret Commonwealth.

Some say that from various places on the highway you can hear the booming bell-like sound and sometimes chimes. Weird lights have been observed and if an automobile engine stops, it will not start again while the bell rings.

"I don't know about all that," skier McKillop said, "but I have seen a light. My wife and I were driving on California 97 near the base of the mountain when we saw a huge beam of light coming out of the mountain. As a kid I had heard stories, but I never expected to see anything like this."

Since 1955 thousands of people from all parts of the world have traveled to the town of Mount Shasta each August to witness the pageant presented by the followers of the I Am Activity of the Saint Germain Foundation.

For many years these followers were looked upon by their more staid neighbors with suspicion and resentment, but eventually the beauty of their doctrines, based on universal energy and power from above, won acceptance.

In 1930 C. W. Ballard, founder of the foundation that grew to have more than twelve million members, was sent to Northern California on government business. In his leisure time he wandered on the mountain, interested in unraveling rumors of The Brotherhood of Sach. He fell in love with the mountain and sensed something unusual there. It became a place where he walked, thought, made decisions and found inspiration and peace.

One day he met there a man who he realized was no ordinary person. The man was, Ballard said, the living, tangible presence of the Master, Saint Germain. Through Ballard the instructions Saint Germain gave on the mountain became decrees and doctrines. Ballard wrote "Unveiled Mysteries" in 1934, and directed the work of the I Am Activity of the Saint Germain Foundation, a foundation that was to better the world through constructive ideas and beauty.

Mt. Shasta was virtually unknown to the world until Peter Skene Ogden, trapper for the Hudson Bay Company, recorded its presence in 1827. Spanish explorers had mentioned a "very high hill, Jesus Maria" and Russian explorers settling at Bodega had talked of "Tshastal" which means the white, or pure mountain.

In 1854 a man named E. D. Pearce led a party of eight to the top of the mountain where they raised an American flag. The following year I. S. Diehl made the first solo climb and placed a temperance banner by the side of the flag. In 1861 W. S. Moses, Yreka, climbed to the top to use instruments loaned by the Smithsonian Institution to make the first measurement of height.

In 1875 a geodetic monument, an unmanned signal device connecting long lines of the main triangulation of the Coast and Geodetic Survey, was located on top of the mountain. In 1903 the monument, heavy and well anchored, toppled and fell near the south base of summit pinnacle.

Why? No one knows.

Each summer groups of amateur archaeologists and occultists visit Mt. Shasta seeking evidence of the elusive Lemurians, signs of the Mystic Brotherhood of Sach, the Yaktayvians, and proof of other legends — and each winter skiers flock to the slopes of the mystic mountain, but the mighty mountain guards its secrets well, if, indeed, secrets it has.

Lonely as God and white as the winter moon, Mt. Shasta remains California's mystery mountain.

NOTES

CHRONOLOGY

Buckhorn Springs .... Pre-1800s Indian sacred place

Mt. Shasta .... 1827 Peter Skene Ogden records presence of mountain

Applegate Trail .... 1846 Southern route established into Oregon Territory

Bear Creek .... 1851 Jimmy Stuart killed, stream named Stuart Creek

Maryum's Rose .... 1851 McKee, Bowen wagons arrived

Jacksonville .... 1852 Gold discovered on Jackson Creek, tent city developed

Jackson County .... 1852 Established in southwestern corner of Oregon Territory

Ashland .... 1852 Founded

Table Rock Treaty .... 1853 Treaty with Indians signed

Fort Lane .... 1853 Military post built in Rogue River Valley

Colver Home .... 1853 Sam and Huldah Colver built house

Dunn Home .... 1854 Patrick Dunn and Mary Hill married

Phoenix .... 1854 Founded

Chavner Home .... 1850s Tom Chavner prepared for visit of missionary priest

Grizzly Peak .... 1855 H. H. Chapman mauled by grizzly bear

Birdseye Home .... 1856 David Birdseye built house

Oregon .... 1859 Oregon achieved statehood

Fort Klamath .... 1861 Military post built during Civil War

Butte Creek Mill .... 1872 Flour mill built on Little Butte Creek

Eagle Point .... 1872 Post office established

Climax .... 1870s Homesteaders settled mountain country

Rogue River .... 1880s Founded as Woodville; name changed 1912

Talent .... 1880s Town platted

Union Creek .... 1880s Wayside built on road to Fort Klamath

Prospect .... 1882 Founded

Medford .... 1883 Founded

Gold Hill .... 1884 Founded

Buck Rock Tunnel .... 1884 Construction started

Central Point .... 1889 Incorporated

Colestin Springs .... 1890s Resort flourished

Blue Ledge Mine .... 1906 Copper mining

Toketee Falls .... 1920s Area explored for hydro electric power

Shale City .... 1922 Oil from rock venture

ABOUT NOT GETTING LOST

With words and artwork we've done the best we can, but because back-country road grids can change from time to time when new access roads are built or old roads are abandoned, we recommend you carry with you an official map that has been drawn-to-scale any time you leave paved and maintained roads. A Metsker's Jackson County map, a current Bureau of Land Management map, or a United States Geological Survey map are best. We cannot be responsible for road conditions or for signing. Before you start out check your gas guage and your tires. Remember you are in logging country and you could encounter logging trucks. Take reasonable precautions and Southern Oregon is yours to enjoy.

PICTURE INDEX

PICTURE INDEX

SOURCE MATERIAL

The books, documents and newspapers listed as source material may be found in the Southern Oregon Historical Society archives, Jacksonville, or in the Ashland Library.

Chapter

 1 Vincent, Dale, Dozier, Phil, Personal Interviews.

 2 Helfrich, Devere, *The Applegate Trail*. Klamath Echoes, No. 9, 1971.

 3 Walling, A. G., *History Of Southern Oregon*, 1884. Bancroft, Hubert Howe, *Bancroft's History Of Oregon*, Volume 2, 1848-1888. McArthur, Lewis A., *Oregon Geographic Names,* Fourth Edition.

 4 McKee family biographical file, Southern Oregon Historical Society archives.

 5 Dunn, Mary Hill, *Undaunted Pioneers, Ever Moving Onward and Homeward,* Valley Printing Company, Eugene, Oregon, 1929.

 6 Walling, A. G., *History Of Southern Oregon*, 1884.

 7 Colver family biographical file, Southern Oregon Historical Society archives.

 8 Helms, Marjorie Neill, *Early Days In Phoenix, Oregon,* Phoenix Community Club, 1954.

 9 Chapman Publishing Company, *Portrait and Biographical Record of Western Oregon,* Chicago, 1904.

10 Thompson, Mrs. (Ruth) Chavner, Personal Interview.

11 Birdseye, Mrs. (Effie) Wesley, Personal Interview.

12 Stone, Buena Cobb, *Fort Klamath,* Royal Publishing Company, General Book Publishers, Dallas, Texas, 1964.

13 Crandall, Peter, Personal Interview.
    Putman, George Francis, Personal Interview.

14 Wertz, Mrs. (Mable) Lester, Personal Interview.
    Applegate, Mrs. (Minnie) Charles, Personal Interview.
    McArthur, Lewis A., *Oregon Geographic Names,* Fourth Edition.

15 Union Creek, Southern Oregon Historical Society archives.

16 Lawrence, Mark, *Buck Rock Tunnel and the Oregon and California Railroad over the Siskiyou Summit,* Research paper, Southern Oregon Historical Society archives.

17 Rawlings, Alice, Personal Interview.
    Colestin, Southern Oregon Historical Society archives.

18 Medford (Oregon) Mail Tribune, 1906-1919.
    Blue Ledge Mine, Southern Oregon Historical Society archives.

19 Boyle, John C., Personal Interview.
    Boyle, John C., *Toketee,* Klocker Printery, Medford, 1977.

20 Ashland Daily Tidings, 1922-1930.

21 Bell, Jim, Personal Interview.

22 Hoover, Charles C., Personal Interview.

23 LePineac, Marcel, Personal Interview.

24 Eichorn, Arthur Francis Sr., *The Mount Shasta Story,* Mt. Shasta Herald, Mt. Shasta, California, 1957.

ACKNOWLEDGMENT

The stories selected for the *Southern Oregon Short Trips Into History* collection are stories I enjoyed researching and writing for the Medford Mail Tribune during the time (1964-1973) I worked for the newspaper as Regional Editor, reporter and feature writer. I sincerely appreciate the Tribune's willingness to see the stories presented now in book form. My appreciation also goes to Marjorie Edens for her support for the book, and to Eva Laufer, Doug Smith, David Pollard and Bill Graham for their interest and help in the design. For thoughtful editing, I thank Anne Thomas, and for map drawings Don Thomas. For providing additional details and for re-reading for accuracy, I am indebted to Ruth Thompson, Nita Birdseye, Mark Lawrence, Claud Hoover; for the loan of pictures, Ruth Thompson, Margaret Joy, Glenn Munsell, M. Bud Hoover and John Bell; for helping me find pictures in the archives of the Southern Oregon Historical Society, Juanita Mayfield, Bob O'Harra and Linda Wiesen.